The Wreck of the Saginaw

The Account Left by Her Captain,

Montgomery Sicard

The Wreck of the Saginaw

October 29, 1870

The account left by her Captain,

Montgomery Sicard

from The Last Cruise of the Saginaw by George H. Read

Cornelia Bagg Srey
Pyara Bagg Sandhu

*Copyright © 2017
by Cornelia Srey, Lang Srey and Pyara Sandhu, Writers, Inc.
First Edition, Christmas, 2017*

Published by

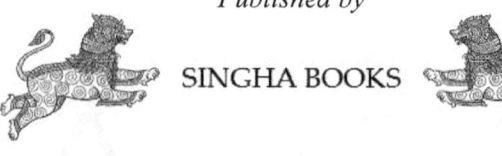

SINGHA BOOKS

All rights reserved, including the right to reproduce this book or portions thereof in any form whatsoever (except for the following, which are public domain: The Last Cruise of the Saginaw by G. H. Read; illustrations, maps and photos from the Library of Congress and the U.S. Geographical Survey)

*Book design by Cornelia Bagg Srey
Cover photo by Lang Srey*

For more information or to book an event,
please contact the authors through *www.TheSmellofWater.com.*

Library of Congress Control Number: 2017917850
Cornelia Srey Lang Srey and Pyara Sandhu Writers Inc., Oakley, CA
ISBN-13: 978-0-692-98037-8 (paperback)

Also by Cornelia Bagg Srey:

With Lang Srey, The Smell of Water –
a twelve-year-old soldier's escape from the Khmer Rouge army
and his determination to stay alive (2014)
ISBN 978-0-692-40750-9

and the sequel, No Front Line –
Searching for Home in a War Zone (2017)
ISBN 978-0-692-86741-9

A Pocket Guide to Cambodian Silk (2016)
ISBN 978-0-692-85302-3

Previous page - the Saginaw at Mare Island Navy Yard, circa 1860

For Egbert Bagg, IV
and Caroline Aldrich Bagg, his mother
who passed Montgomery Sicard's manuscript
down to us

OUR MOST HEARTFELT THANKS TO:

Hans Konrad Van Tilburg, Ph.D.

for A Civil War Gunboat in Pacific Waters –
Life on Board USS *Saginaw*

without his book, we couldn't have written this one

Dean King, John B. Hattendorf and J. Worth Estes

for A Sea of Words –
A Lexicon and Companion for Patrick O'Brian's Seafaring Tales

without their book, we wouldn't have understood
Montgomery Sicard's manuscript and George Henry Read's account

*Joyce Giles (Museum Manager)
and Barbara Davis (Museum Librarian)*
both volunteers at the Mare Island Historic Park

for graciously giving us access to the Museum's files,
and for their encouragement

Lang Srey

for technical advice,
several laptops,
and endless encouragement

"To the north-west of the Hawaiian Islands, for a distance of over one thousand miles, stretches a succession of coral reefs and shoals, with here and there a sandy islet thrown up by the winds and waves..."
— Anonymous survivor of the wreck of the Saginaw

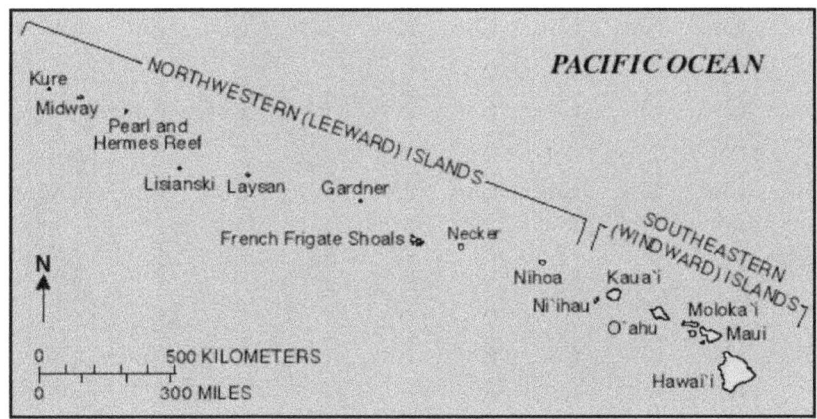

United States Geographical Survey
The Hawaiian Islands

An *atoll* is a coral reef enclosing a lagoon. Most atolls in the Hawaiian chain have formed on the submerged rim of the caldera of an old volcano (the lagoon is the flooded caldera).

A *shoal* is a shallow spot in the water, less than 36 feet deep (usually a sandbar).

The U.S.S. Saginaw's mission in 1870 was to carry blasting contractors to one of three islands in the *Midway Atoll ("the Midways"),* keep them supplied with powder and provisions, and supervise their work.

After leaving the Midways, the Saginaw wrecked on *Kure Atoll.* There is one island inside the reef, *Green Island.* In 1870, it was known as *Ocean Island.* It is the most remote island in the Hawaiian chain.

At that time the Hawaiian Islands were also called the *Sandwich Islands,* named by the explorer Captain James Cook for the promoter of his voyage, the fourth Earl of Sandwich. Cook discovered and charted the islands in 1778, just 92 years before the Saginaw set out for them.

Table of Contents

The Story Behind *The Wreck of the Saginaw*	1
A Nineteenth-century Map of the Pacific Ocean	6
The Saginaw, 1859 to 1869	7
The Saginaw's Mission in 1870	8
The Men Aboard	
At Sailing from San Francisco	9
When the Ship was Wrecked	9
The Lexicon of the Sea	17
The Manuscript in the Secretary Desk	19
A Missing Ship	85
The Court of Inquiry	85
Epilogue	
The Crew	87
The Last Mystery	91
133 Years Later, the Wreck Discovered	91
Destinations	92
George H. Read's *The Last Cruise of the Saginaw*	95
Index, by Crewmember	141

The Story Behind
The Wreck of the Saginaw

In my grandparents' home, guarded on either side by portraits of my ancestors, was a tall and stately secretary desk. The space behind the paned glass doors had been lined with dark green velvet, which, by the time I was born, had faded to the dusky color of lichens. Fastened to the velvet were more portraits, miniatures in oil. But the real treasures were the objects that sat upon the shelves.

The whole of the desk was a reliquary of my grandfather's family's history. Not back to 1635, when a sixteen-year-old blacksmith came from England with nothing more than his trade. But as far back as the 1700's.

As I've said, it was my grandfather's family's history, but its guardian was my grandmother. On visits when the afternoon was quiet she'd open the cabinet and take things down, one by one, for me to marvel at. The flying fish wing brought back by a sea captain, in the days when New Englanders didn't know there were fish that could fly. My great-great-grandmother's seal, with "Cornelia" etched into it so her friends would know from the wax on the flap of the envelope who had sent them a letter. My great-grandmother's glass-and-silver perfume bottles. My grandfather's invitation to the White House, for his contributions to early twentieth-century architecture. The Inuit carving of an owl, brought back by my father from one of his Canadian hunting trips. The most prized possessions of each generation had been added one by one, and had gradually filled the cabinet. But by some magic of my grandmother's, there was always room for one thing more.

Among the treasures in the drawers of the desk was a genealogy, compiled by my great grandfather. And a thin, papery manuscript, dated 1885.

The author's name was nowhere on the manuscript, but there was a name on the last page. Montgomery Sicard. It was his account of the wreck of a vessel under his command, the U. S. S. Saginaw – a steamer fitted with sails. It was my father who took the manuscript out of the desk to show to me, once I was old enough to read it. He told me that he thought it had been published years ago.

But no one ever *checked*.

Fifty years later I published my first book, The Smell of Water – my husband's account of his escape from the Khmer Rouge army in 1979. I had worked for six years on the story, sometimes sixteen hours a day. Now, I found myself in a strange void, and my mind wandered in and out of the stories I'd heard of others who had survived the unsurvivable. And I remembered Captain Sicard. I decided to check to see if his manuscript *had* ever been published.

First, I checked Amazon online. Ah. The account of the wreck of the Saginaw had been published in 1912. So my father had been right.

But wait... the book on my screen had been published by George H. Read. Not Montgomery Sicard. Who the *heck* was George Read?

I carefully opened the manuscript that had lain for five generations in the secretary desk, and read the list of the officers of the Saginaw. And there he was – the paymaster.

I started to read the published text online. The chapter titles didn't match the manuscript in my hand. Well, the editor had changed them. And then I began to read the text... This was a different account! Had Captain Sicard's manuscript ever even been copyrighted?

I checked the U. S. Government's copyright website, and had my answer within half an hour. No – it had not.

I also found George Read's original 1912 book – not the republished version I had been reading on the Amazon site. I clicked it open, and there was a photograph of the stately Captain Sicard. I had never seen a picture of him. And then I read that *he* had drawn most of the illustrations in George Read's book!

So why had he written his account, if he had not intended to publish it? Oh. Of course. The Saginaw was a naval vessel, he was a naval officer, and the ship had been lost under his command. He had to write a report for the naval Board of Inquiry.

But his account was a *fabulous* story – I couldn't put it down. It *had* to be published.

I immediately texted my son, a history buff, Marine Biology major and weekend diver. I sent him the link to the NOAA website of the atoll where the ship had gone down, and when he saw the underwater stills of the wreck, well, he was in. We set to work.

The first thing we did was find out how we were related to Montgomery Sicard. We opened the copy of the genealogy that my father had made for me, spread it out on the dining room table, and found the last page written in the nineteenth century. The first thing that caught my eye was my own name, "Cornelia" – my great-great grandmother. My son and I were sitting next to her silver tea tray, passed down to me because I had been named after her. With my finger I traced the line from her name to her children's, and there was my great grandfather – the compiler of the genealogy. And then we looked for "Montgomery". But there were *nine* men on the page with that first name. Ah – there he was. My great grandfather had thought to write, "Rear Admiral, U.S. Navy" (the captain's rank at the time he retired) under his name. Montgomery Sicard was his first cousin.

My son and I started typing furiously, recreating the manuscript in Microsoft Word. Using the font closest to the original, and preserving each linguistic quirk and spelling no longer in use. We got George Read's account of the shipwreck, and read that, too. We lingered over the line drawings – our manuscript had none. So we copied each one, and inserted them into our newly-typed version. We couldn't wait to publish.

Not so fast. Captain Sicard's account wouldn't make any *sense* to a reader today. His world, in 1870, was a very different one than the one we live in. I began to read the manuscript again, and again, to be sure that *I* understood it. Before trying to explain it to someone else.

Their destination, a tiny island halfway across the Pacific Ocean, was like the edge of the world in 1870. Rescue was a great uncertainty, should anything happen to them.

Let me tell you, the phrase, "sailing into uncharted waters" has survived into the twenty-first century for a *reason*. They would have to go back and forth from Honolulu to the Midways several times, nearly the full length of the Northwestern Hawaiian chain. But this area had been only roughly charted; at least nine whalers had wrecked there. And, in those days, not all sailors knew how to swim.

And then there was disease. On their last mission, more than one third of the crew had contracted yellow fever; a vaccine would not be available for another seventy years. One man had died – the ship's doctor. The one man most able to help the others. And before their mission in the Midways was complete, one seaman would die of cholera.

Then there was the chronology of the captain's career. We didn't understand it at all. He had joined the Navy at... *15?* Yes, his father had died when he was four, but his mother had moved her children upstate to Utica in order to be near her family. Montgomery Sicard would have grown up with my great grandfather. We were a well-to-do family in the nineteenth century, and his uncle was a Supreme Court justice; he wouldn't have *had* to enlist. My son remembered his Marine Biology courses. "No computers back then, no Internet, no 'automatic' anything. Think of all he would have had to learn, Mom. Navigation and astronomy. Oceanography, including winds, tides and currents. Drawing, charting and cartography. Marine biology. Communications. International law, marine law, and U. S. Navy law. Sailing, rigging, and sailmaking. How a steam engine works. Personnel management, in order to run an entire ship. Resource management, to economize on the use of coal and make sure the ship's food and fresh water didn't run out. And a hundred other things. Anyone wanting to be an officer would have had to start his studies very early." More research revealed that he had graduated from the Naval Academy at Annapolis at 19. And first took command of a ship at 28; he was on the fast track. Still more research explained why – promising young officers moved up the ranks quickly during the four years of the Civil War.

And then we started counting. Backwards, from October 29, 1870. We had assumed that the commander of such a critical mission would be an older man. But when the Saginaw went down, Montgomery Sicard was just 34 years old. And the father of two young children – a daughter, four, and a son, two.

We started comparing dates again. When the Saginaw wrecked, and when she was due back in San Francisco. A difference of 33 days. By the time anyone realized that the crew was missing, it might be too late to rescue them. And they were not at the Midways, their declared departure point – they were at Ocean Island, fifty miles away. Any rescue party would be looking for them *in the wrong place*. In 1870, there had been no way to communicate their detour to the Navy.

This explained another mystery – why they had gone to Ocean Island at all. The captain had no reason to believe that there was anyone shipwrecked there. But he wanted to be *sure*. It was the communication issue again. Ocean Island was even more remote than the Midways, and the survivors of the last ship to wreck there had waited *seven months* to be rescued. Sicard's plan had been to circle the atoll once, searching for signs of survivors with a spyglass, and then turn around and return to San Francisco.

Then I discovered something else. And once again, it was in the dates. In our manuscript, the departure from San Francisco was said to be the 14th of May. But in all of the historical records, it was the 22nd of February. Our manuscript had been written by someone who had not originally been part of the crew – someone who had signed on in Hawaii. What we had thought was Montgomery Sicard's account was not written by Montgomery Sicard at all!

So... where was *his* account? In the end, we decided that he never wrote one. After preparing all of the reports for his superiors and the naval Court of Inquiry, we think he just didn't want to write any more. And although he believed that he was not responsible for the accident, the fate of the Saginaw party must have weighed heavily on him. But he would have wanted his family, including his extended family, to know exactly what had happened. And that he had been exonerated by the Court of Inquiry. Thus the manuscript in the secretary desk. Given to his cousin, and passed down to the next generation, and the next, with the desk. And there was now no doubt in our minds why he had never *published* an account. He would not have wanted to profit, or appear to profit, from the loss of the lives of members of his crew.

So why didn't he give a copy of George Read's account to my great grandfather? It was much more comprehensive. We think he didn't have it – Read's account wasn't published until 1912, more than a decade after the captain's death.

So many mysteries. Solved, now. But there was one left.

The commander was an extremely intelligent man, exceptionally meticulous, and careful, in everything that he did. And he knew that two ships had already wrecked on Ocean Island, and eight had wrecked on the Midway he was just leaving. But he didn't know why.

He had set their course so that the Saginaw's approach to Ocean Island would be after sunrise, when the reefs could be seen in time to avoid them. And he had gone on deck at 2:15 a.m. to personally monitor their progress, their speed, the steam pressure, and the set of the sails. Yet the Saginaw hit at 3:22 in the morning. Even the Court of Inquiry couldn't understand why the accident had happened. Until Commander Sicard explained it to them – he was the only one to ever figure it out.

Cornelia Bagg Srey

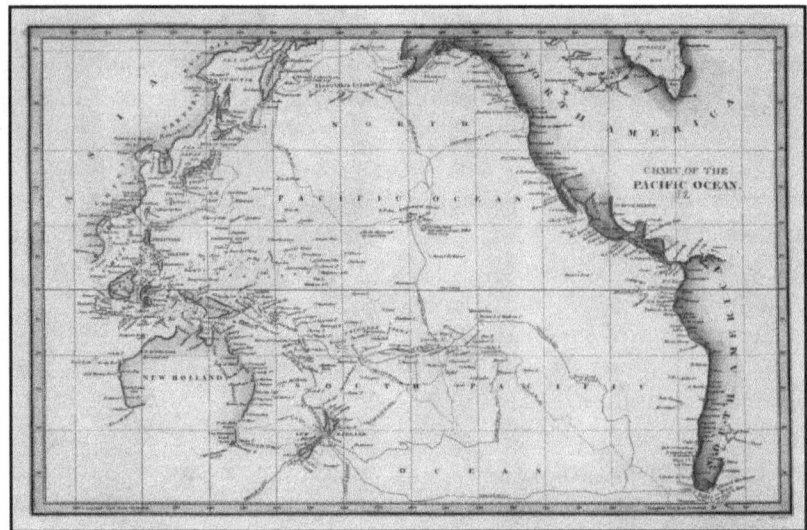

United States Library of Congress

A NINETEENTH-CENTURY MAP OF THE PACIFIC OCEAN

The parallel of latitude that runs horizontally across the center of the map marks the equator – 0 degrees latitude.

The meridian that runs vertically down the center marks the 160-degree meridian.

The "Sandwich Isles" are on this meridian, 20 degrees (on this map, one square) above the equator. So the Island of Hawai'i, at 19 degrees latitude and 155 degrees longitude, has been drawn in the right place.

The Midways, however, at 28 degrees north and 177 degrees west, are not even on the map.

THE SAGINAW, 1859 TO 1869

The U. S. S. Saginaw was the first ship to be built in the first naval shipyard on the West Coast – Mare Island Navy Yard, just northeast of San Francisco.

She was to play a critical part in a maverick new nation's endeavor to continue pushing west. America had won its independence just 76 years earlier, and had acquired the 2.14-kilometer Louisiana Purchase only 56 years before. The Gold Rush was in its 11th year, and the State of California was only 9 years old. Alaska was still a Russian colony, owned by the Czar. But in the Hawaiian Islands, with Kamehameha IV on the throne, international commerce flourished. Ships could be reprovisioned in Honolulu, and go on from there to the other side of the *world*. It was an exciting time to be an American.

And so, the Saginaw was designed to traverse the open ocean. She would serve in the China Seas. She was rigged as a sailing ship, but given a second means of propulsion – a steam engine that turned a paddle wheel on either side of the hull. But remember, this was 158 years ago. She was a *small* vessel, just 47.2 meters (155 feet) from stem to stern and 7.92 meters (26 feet) in breadth, designed for a crew of only 59 men.

She sailed from San Francisco in 1860 for Shanghai. The Second Opium War had just ended, and in its aftermath, the Taiping Rebellion and reaction to the coolie trade and the opening of more ports to Westerners made Chinese coastal waters unsafe. As part of the Navy's East India Squadron, the Saginaw's mission was to protect American citizens and suppress pirate activity. Her territory extended as far south as Vietnam and as far north as Japan.

But the United States had a war of its own. After returning to Mare Island for repairs in 1862, the Saginaw was assigned to the Pacific Squadron to thwart Confederate activity up and down the Pacific Coast. This took her to ports in Mexico and Central America, where she also protected the interests of the United States endangered by European interference in Mexico. She even escorted steamers carrying cargoes of bullion from the California gold fields.

Upon the end of the Civil War, the Saginaw was employed in the push to new frontiers. In 1866 she sailed to Puget Sound in Washington, and aided Western Union in laying a cable that brought the first telegraphic service to the region. The United States purchased Alaska in 1867, and the following year, the Saginaw explored and charted the Alaskan coast.

In 1869 command of the ship was transferred to Lieutenant Commander Montgomery Sicard. His first assignment was to survey a navigational hazard off the western coast of Mexico. More than one third of the crew contracted yellow fever. The steam engine failed, and the ship proceeded north up the coast under sail. The voyage was so prolonged that, when the Saginaw finally reached San Francisco, only a half day's provisions remained. She returned to Mare Island for repairs.

THE SAGINAW'S MISSION IN 1870

In the middle of the nineteenth century tea was king, and sailing ships – clippers – made the journey from Western Europe and the East Coast of the United States to China to get it. But although very fast, clippers were narrow for their length – their capacity to carry bulk freight was limited.

So commercial steamships were employed. But the distance between Atlantic ports and China was up to 28,000 kilometers (17,000 miles); construction of the Suez Canal was not started until 1859. No steamship could carry enough coal to make this voyage nonstop and still have enough space left to carry a commercial cargo. Sailing ships remained the vessels best suited to the tea trade.

The completion of the American Transcontinental Railroad in 1869 meant that tea could be got to Atlantic markets via Pacific routes to and from China. Commercial steamers were once again employed, and a coaling station was established at Honolulu.

But Honolulu was out of the way. The U. S. Congress appropriated $50,000 for blasting a shipping channel through the coral reef surrounding one of the Midway Islands – 1100 miles northwest of Honolulu – so that a coaling station could be established there. The Saginaw was detailed to carry the crew of blasting contractors to the island, keep them provisioned, monitor their progress, and bring them back to San Francisco when the channel had been completed.

She sailed under the Golden Gate for Honolulu on February 22, 1870, rolling and pitching in a dense fog, the wind howling through her rigging – straight into a stiff southeaster. And this is how her last voyage began.

The Men Aboard

At Sailing from San Francisco

Bound for the Midways were the captain, his navigators, a coxswain (helmsman), a boatswain (in charge of all deck activity, including handling the sails), quartermasters (who assisted with steering, navigation and signaling), engineers, medical personnel, the paymaster, yeomen (in charge of stores), coal heavers, firemen, a blacksmith, cooks and stewards, carpenters, seamen, landsmen (who performed basic tasks such as hauling and hoisting) and a 12-man armed marine guard.

The crew was a multinational one, from the U.S., England, Ireland, Scotland, Canada, France, Belgium, Denmark, Sweden, Finland, Germany, Austria, Poland, Greenland, Jamaica, Barbados, Peru, Nicaragua and the Philippines. 16 crewmen were black, or mixed. The captain would recruit more men in Hawaii.

All of the officers had been through the Civil War, and all but the captain were under 30. Most of them knew each other from the Naval Academy.

When the ship was wrecked

"The following is a list of the officers and crew of the Saginaw as it appeared on the pay-roll at the time she was wrecked; I feel that I should name them all in recognition of a comradeship in suffering never to be forgotten where each one performed his duty unflinchingly."

George H. Read

Officers

Montgomery Sicard, Lieutenant Commander
John G. Talbot, Lieutenant
J. K. Cogswell, Perry Garst, and A. H. Parsons, Ensigns
George H. Read, Passed Assistant Paymaster
James Butterworth, Passed Assistant Engineer
H. C. Blye, Passed Asst. Engineer (in charge of contractor's party)
George H. Robinson, Master's Mate
John J. Ryan, C. D. Foss, Herschel Main, Jones Godfrey, Second Assistant Engineers

Petty Officers

Peter Francis, Quartermaster
Nicholas Barton, Quartermaster
Thomas Hayes, Sailor's Mate
John Lane, Boatswain's Mate
James Foschack, Gunner's Mate
J. M. Logan, Yeoman
William Halford, Coxswain
Samuel A. Thompson, Master at Arms
Charles Hale, Paymaster's Yeoman
A. E. Myfinger, Cabin Steward
Solomon Graves, Cabin Cook
Joseph Ross, Wardroom Steward
George D. Wauchoss, Wardroom Cook
Henry B. Clark, Third-class Apothecary
William Edman, Ship's Cook
Henry Wallace, Steerage Steward
L. McCabe, Steerage Cook

Francis Scott, Lorenzo Coburg, George White, First-class Firemen
George Hubert, Second-class Fireman

William Cairns, Michael Lynch, Henry D. Vivian, Daniel Collins, Seamen
Joseph A. Bailey, John H. Wallace, Dennis A. Fitzgerald, John Daley, Charles Brown, Dennis M. Hayes, Michael Jordan, Edward James, Ordinary Seamen

James Nichols, W. J. Evans, Edward O'Brien, Thomas Kearney, J. R. Miller, Martin Doran, William Fallon, Thomas Larkin, Joseph McLaughlin, George Saunders, William Combs, Joseph A. Agarrie, Michael Garvey, John Murphy, John Downs, James McNamara, John Riley, Thomas Melody, James M. Nolan, Landsmen

Marine Guard

Charles A. Martin, Orderly Sargent
John G. Moore, Corporal
Phillip Morris, Corporal

Privates

D. G. Brennan
Thomas Wiseman
David Muir
James Sarsfield
Thomas Jones
John McGrath
Lewis Peck

George Read's list is of the Saginaw's crew, numbering 75 men. It should have included Adam Frank, the ship's doctor.

The contractor's party was comprised of 12 men:

George A. Bailey
J. Henry Russell
William G. Loring
Charles H. Mitchell
Jon C. Toumey
Joseph Battersby
Charles Collins
James Muir
John Brown
Frank Quigley
E. P. Judd
Edward Cahill

This is only 88 men, but our manuscript says that 93 were aboard when the ship hit the reef. Dr. Hans Konrad Van Tilburg, in <u>A Civil War Gunboat in Pacific Waters</u>, also says there were 93 on board. The 5 men missing from this list may have been part of the marine guard (12 men, when they left San Francisco).

But do the numbers really matter? Yes, they do. Because the ship had been designed for a crew of *59*. And she would have been carrying provisions for the extra 34 men as well. A 58 percent overload – before adding the heavy contractor's equipment, some of which had to be lashed to the deck.

LIEUTENANT COMMANDER MONTGOMERY SICARD

from The Last Cruise of the Saginaw, by George H. Read

*The captain of the Saginaw,
around the time he assumed command of her.*

Montgomery Sicard was born to Lydia Hunt of Utica, New York and Stephen Sicard of Philadelphia in New York City in 1836.

He graduated from the United States Naval Academy at Annapolis in 1855, at the age of 19. He was made a midshipman in the Home Squadron. He passed the lieutenant's exam and was promoted to Sailing Master (navigator) three years later. He received his commission as Lieutenant in 1860, a year before the Civil War, and thereafter served aboard steam sloops. He was part of the capture of New Orleans in 1862, after which he was promoted to Lieutenant Commander. On shore leave in 1863 he married Elizabeth Floyd, a descendant of one of the signers of the Declaration of Independence. The following year he commanded the Seneca in two assaults on Fort Fisher. He became an instructor at the Naval Academy at Annapolis in 1866. Two years later he took command of the steam sloop Pensacola in the North Atlantic Squadron, and in 1869, he took command of the Saginaw in the Pacific Squadron.

LIEUTENANT JOHN GUNNELL TALBOT

from The Last Cruise of the Saginaw, by George H. Read

*Second in command on the Saginaw,
Lieutenant Talbot was the ship's executive officer.*

John Gunnell Talbot was born in Danville, Kentucky, in 1844.

He was made a midshipman in 1862, graduated from the United States Naval Academy at Annapolis in 1866, and was commissioned Ensign in 1868, Master in 1869 and Lieutenant in 1870.

Talbot was 26 when the Saginaw was wrecked. The next day he came to the captain and told him that, if a boat were to be sent for help, he wanted to be the officer in charge.

ASSISTANT ENGINEER JAMES BUTTERWORTH

from The Last Cruise of the Saginaw, by George H. Read

Another of the Saginaw's promising officers, James Butterworth

The work of a meticulous engineer can save as many lives as any act of valor. It was James Butterworth's ability to improvise quickly that would save the Saginaw's crew in those first critical days on Ocean Island.

Born in Rochdale, England, he had served in the U.S. Navy for more than 8 years before sailing out of San Francisco with Sicard and his crew in 1870.

He was 29 when the Saginaw was wrecked.

SECOND ASSISTANT ENGINEER HERSCHEL MAIN

Like James Butterworth, Herschel Main was a skilled and experienced engineer. His ability to improvise would enable John Talbot, William Halford, Peter Francis, John Andrews and James Muir to complete their mission.

He had enlisted in the Navy in the Civil War, and later graduated from the United States Naval Academy at Annapolis.

He was 24 when the Saginaw was wrecked.

COXSWAIN WILLIAM HALFORD

from The Last Cruise of the Saginaw, by George H. Read

The ship's helmsman, around the time he joined the Saginaw.

William Halford was born in Gloucestershire, England, in 1841. He enlisted in the United States Navy in 1869, and joined the crew of the Saginaw.

Halford was 29 when she was wrecked.

QUARTERMASTER PETER FRANCIS

From Manila, Peter Francis was half Filipino and half Spanish. His position as quartermaster typically involved assisting with steering, navigation and signaling.

He had served with William Halford on the U.S.S. Independence.

Contractors John Andrews and James Muir

Andrews and Muir were large Boston hard-hat divers hired to blast the reef at the Midways. Andrews was 38 when the Saginaw was wrecked. Muir was 36; he was originally from Glasgow, Scotland.

Paymaster George Henry Read

George Read was born in Philadelphia in 1843.

He served on board the U.S.S. Pocahontas at the beginning of the Civil War, taking part in the capture of Port Royal in 1861. He spent the rest of the war on blockade duty.

He was 27 when the Saginaw was wrecked.

He is said to have been gentlemanly, affable and kind. And he seems to have been an optimist.

His account is eloquently written – much more engaging than the account handed down to us. It's also more complete.

But did his optimism *color* the story? His cheery tone is actually the reason we decided to publish the manuscript in the drawer of my grandparents' desk.

Because Read was an officer, his life on Ocean Island was marginally more comfortable than that of the seamen. He had known most of his fellow officers for years. And he was one of the lucky few who didn't get very sick. Combine this with the optimism that seems to have been his nature, and his account paints a different picture than does ours.

As I've said, our manuscript was written by someone who had signed on in Hawaii. Looking at what information he did and didn't have, he was not an officer. And because he was a late addition to the crew, he probably didn't have many friends among them. His account is much more somber than Read's, and, we think, mirrors the mood of most of the shipwrecked men. He didn't mention Christmas, and by the start of the new year, had stopped writing altogether. He deferred to someone else's account for the conclusion of the story.

The Lexicon of the Sea

The Saginaw and her small boats:

cutter	a boat fitted for rowing and sailing, used to carry light stores and passengers
dinghy	the smallest of the Saginaw's boats, a rowboat
gig	a light, narrow boat fitted either for rowing or sailing, generally used by the commander
launch	the largest of the Saginaw's boats, a long, low sailing vessel suitable for a short cruise
scow	a large, flat-bottomed rowboat (used by the blasting contractors at Midway Island)
sloop	a small sailing ship-of-war (the Saginaw was a steam sloop, a two-masted brig)

A sloop's parts and equipment:

bilge	The lowest internal part of the hull
bow	the forward part of the ship, beginning where the planks arch inward and ending at the stem
clewed up	a sail's lower ends drawn up to the yard or mast (the opposite of "furled")
guy	a rope, chain or rod used to guide and steady something being hoisted, such as a mast
hurricane deck	the upper deck
keel	the lowest longitudinal timber of a vessel, on which the frame is built up
log line	a line of 100 fathoms (600 feet) or more used to calculate the speed of a ship
quarter deck	the deck from which the captain, master (responsible for navigation and sailing) or officer of the watch commands sailing activities
rod	a measure of length equal to 16.5 feet
sextant	a navigational instrument that measures the angular distance of objects
shrouds	large ropes that provide lateral support to the masts, enabling them to carry sail
spar	the poles in a vessel's rigging, such as the masts and yards
speaking-tube	a pipe used to convey vocal communications to various parts of a ship

stem	the curved upright bow timber of a vessel, into which the planks of the bow are joined
stern	the rear of the vessel
yard	a long, narrow wooden pole slung horizontally from the mast to support the sails

Directional terms:

aft, abaft	toward the stern of the vessel
lee	the side of a vessel away from the wind
port, larboard	the left-hand side of the vessel, looking forward (toward the bow)
starboard	the right-hand side of the vessel, looking forward (toward the bow)

Sailing terms used by Halford in his narrative:

by the wind	as near as possible to the direction from which the wind is blowing
hauled	to change course, sail a certain course, or pull
heeled	leaned to one side; a ship normally heels in the wind
hove to	brought the boat to a standstill without anchoring
stood to	held a course for (such as, "stood to sea" or "stood into harbor")

THE MANUSCRIPT IN THE SECRETARY DESK

An Account of the Wreck

of the

U. S. Steamer Saginaw

October 29th, 1870.

--- o ---

'Where lingers he ?

Alive perchance on some lone beach,

Or thirsty Isle, beyond the reach

Of man, he hears the mocking speech

Of wind and sea.'

--- o ---

Buffalo, N. Y.
1885.

OFFICERS OF THE U. S. S. SAGINAW.

--- o ---

Commander,	Montgomery Sicard.
Lieutenant,	John G. Talbot.
Paymaster,	George H. Reed.
Surgeon,	Adam Frank.
Ensign,	A. H. Parsons.
Mate,	George Robinson.

--- o ---

Engineers.

James Butterworth	John J. Ryan.
H. C. Blye.	Herschel Main.
C. D. Ross.	James Godfrey.

Marines, Contractor's party, and Ships' Crew, numbering in all ninety-three men.

--- o ---

CORAL REEFS AND SHOALS.

To the north-west of the Hawaiian Islands, for a distance of over 1,000 miles, stretches a succession of coral reefs and shoals, with here and there a sandy islet, throw up by the winds and waves, and mostly bare of vegetation. These islets are termed 'atolls' by geographers, a word taken from the Maldive language, and signifying a coral island consisting of a strip of coral ring or reef surrounding a central lagoon.

Through the misrepresentation of interested parties, the Pacific Mail Steamship Company was led to believe, that, by the expenditure of a reasonable sum, a good harbor could be made at Midway Island, a barren sand bank, enclosed in a coral reef, situated in north latitude, 23 degrees, 13 minutes, and west longitude 177 degrees and 23 minutes, distant from Honolulu about eleven hundred miles, and forty-eight miles from Ocean Island. This was to be the coaling station for the company's steamers, on their voyages between San Francisco and China. As a commencement, Congress appropriated $ 50,000 for the work of blasting a ship channel through the reef. The Saginaw was detailed for the service. On the 14th of May, the Saginaw sailed for Honolulu, and up to the date of her loss-- October 29-- had made four trips to and from the island.

from The Last Cruise of the Saginaw, by George H. Read

Midway Island as it looked when the crew first landed. Sketch by Montgomery Sicard.

On her last trip from Honolulu, Captain Sicard brought orders to the working party to discontinue operations, as the appropriation ($ 50,000) had been exhausted.

After toiling laboriously and constantly whenever the weather and health of the men permitted, under water and in boats and scows, for six months, using large quantities of powder and fuse, they had excavated a channel about fifteen feet wide and 450 feet in length, and the $ 50,000 was expended, and the work brought to a stop. At this rate the work will cost, when completed, at least the sum of $ 1,000,000.

DEPARTURE OF THE SAGINAW.

Having taken on board the working party and their materials on Friday (traditionally unlucky day for sailors) The Saginaw left Midway Island for San Francisco.

from The Last Cruise of the Saginaw, by George H. Read

Midway Island as the crew left it.

It was determined, however, to visit Ocean Island, about forty-eight miles to the west, where it was possible that some vessel might have been wrecked. The wind was fair, and the engines were running slowly, and it was expected that they would be near the island about 4 in the morning.

A sketch of Kure Atoll, showing Ocean Island

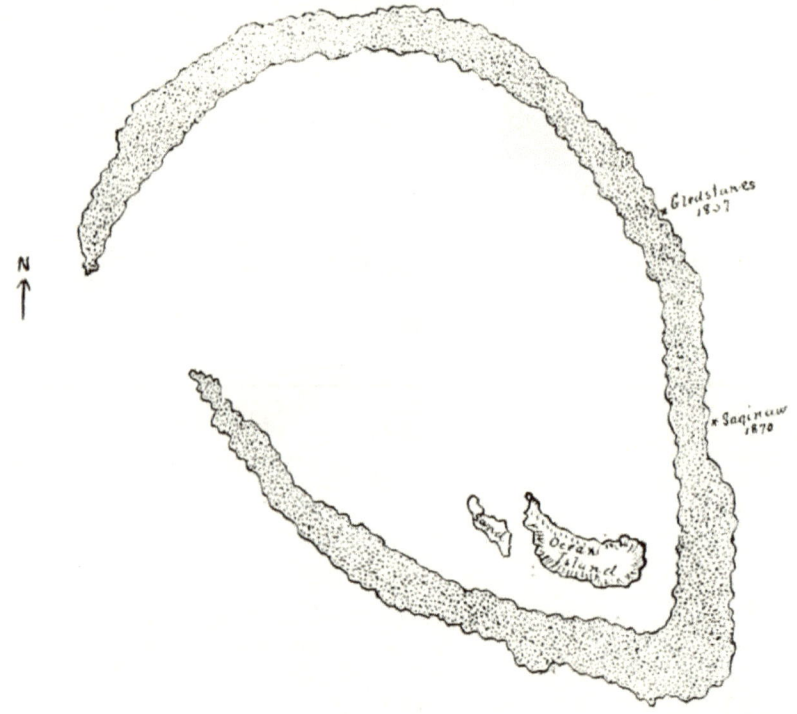

from The Last Cruise of the Saginaw, by George H. Read

The captain of the British whaler Gledstanes, wrecked in 1837, described Ocean Island as about 3 miles in circumference. Where the American whaler Parker wrecked in 1842 is not shown on the sketch above. The sand island west of Ocean Island is where the November 2nd incident would occur.

At 2.30 the engines were stopped entirely. At 3.30 the main on the lookout reported that he saw something ahead which he

THOUGHT TO BE BREAKERS

The orders were given immediately to back the engines, which was done, and continued for about ten minutes, when the wheels refused to move, the difficulty being evidently that some of the steam connections were broken. During this time the top-sails were still set, and could not be got in before she struck.

When the breakers were reported and the engines backed, the men were sent aloft to furl the top-sails, but they were not got in soon enough to prevent their giving the ship more headway than the engines, with the steam they had, could counteract. There were sixteen pounds of steam when the engines were first backed and the fires were banked. Steam was used down to seven pounds, but in the meantime the fires were opened, and at the time the vessel became finally fast in the rocks the steam was rising. The top-sails were all the sails she was carrying at the time of the striking, the foretopsail being only clewed up.

from The Last Cruise of the Saginaw, by George H. Read

The Saginaw after impact, with her bow still on the reef. Sketch by Montgomery Sicard (from memory).

Shortly after striking forward, the ship swung around broad side on, and huge breakers were pounding at her bow and star-board side. As the engine ceased working, she struck under the fire-room, raising the fire-room plates and the star-board boiler.

THE WATER CAME IN TORRENTS, and in a few moments was up to the grate bars. Every wave that struck the ship threatened to break her to pieces. The smoke-stack went over the side, and the ship gradually careened over to port towards the reef. She was being lifted bodily upon the rocks, and in a little time the after part of the vessel was above the water level, so that the men could climb directly from the ship to the rocks without danger. Gangs went to work at once to get provisions out of the fore and main holds.

Not a great deal was obtained from the fore hold, as the forward part of the vessel was not on the rocks, as was the after part, and the hold was full of water. This was before daylight. When day broke an island appeared less than a mile from the ship, surround by the reef.
This was Ocean Island.

BREAKING TO PIECES.

As soon as it was light, the boats were got out and taken over the reef to the lagoon with little or no damage. The ship was evidently going to break up somewhere near the engine, as the forward part of her had already much greater heel than the after, and the deck was to a considerable extent broken up. The water was nearly up to the hatches. Lines of men were formed to carry the provisions that had been saved to the boats. About 7 or 8 O'clock the shop labored so much that main mast was ordered to be cut away. The heel of the vessel was such that the mast broke short off at the deck with simply cutting the shrouds on the star-board side, the mast falling so as to make a gangway to the reef, and so remained until the vessel finally broke up. In a short time the forward part of the ship separated, as it had threatened, just forward of the engines, and swung around against the reef. The mast fell, and very soon that part of the ship lost all resemblance to what it had been.

Very fortunately, a good portion of the provisions were in the after hold and could be got at with comparative ease. The day was spent in saving and conveying to the island what provision, tools, sails, etc., could be got at. But few articles of clothing were saved, and with great difficulty. To add to the disagreeable character of the situation, many of the men became utterly unable to work, on account of drink. In clearing out the hold they had discovered the wine-lockers in the ward-room, and had helped themselves, and although there was nothing in it stronger than ale and claret, on men who are debarred from all liquors and who were fasting, the effect was soon apparent. At 5 o'clock P. M. the word was passed

TO ABANDON THE SHIP.

All hands accordingly went on shore. The damaged provisions were spread out on awnings and such sails as could be got at. Much of the bread had been placed in bags, and the wash of the sea rushing through the holes in the ship's side had reduced it to a mere pulp, such as to be absolutely uneatable, except to people in danger of starvation. The bread in boxes fared better, since it was kept in shape, and was not so throughly saturated. Much of the beef and pork was broken out of the barrels, and everything was adrift. On getting to the shore, tired, wet and hungry, after twenty-four hours of fasting and fourteen of severe labor, no one felt any ambition to provide for a shelter, but sunk to rest in the sand. During the afternoon a party had been in search of fresh water, but had found none. Streams or springs were not expected, but it was thought that by digging, fresh water might be obtained. But this first attempt was a failure. As the sun went down on the ship-wrecked company,

"ON A LONE, BARREN ISLAND,"
quite remote from the route of ocean travel, all hands were piped to supper. A half a cup full of water from the scanty stock saved from the ship, a half cake of hard bread, and a couple ounces of raw pork constituted the allowance per man. The officers--fifteen in number--fared questionable better, for they had a small leg of mutton, which, having been kept too long in a warm climate, was tainted, and had an "ancient and fish-like smell." Some chickens, turkeys and sheep that were saved were turned loose on the island. It was necessary to put all hands --ninety-three

souls-- at once on short allowance, for it was uncertain what supplies the island might afford, and a long period might elapse before they were relieved. After the frugal supper, those who were fortunate enough to have saved tobacco divided, and after a smoke, as cheerfully as the circumstances would allow, all settled their wearied bodies among the bushes, to sleep, or to ponder over the events of the day, and to speculate on the prospects ahead.

HOW THE CREW FARED.

The next day was employed in securing whatever could be got at from the wreck, and digging on the island for water.

from The Last Cruise of the Saginaw, by George H. Read

Salvaging timbers from the wreck. Sketch by Montgomery Sicard.

None was found that was much different in taste from the water from the ocean. One well, only, afforded very brackish and bitter tasting water, which a few could drink without disagreeable effects, while others had to avoid it wholly, or suffer.

Supper consisted of a piece of bread and stewed turtle. So they lay down to rest again in discomfort. Some had obtained mattresses and blankets from the wreck, but they were all wet. They had got ashore a small stationary boiler belong to the contractor's party. This was put upon Monday, the third day after landing, as a distiller, and to the the great joy of all hands, it succeeded admirably in producing fresh water from salt. Fearful of disaster to this invaluable distiller, a watch was set over it, consisting of three of the ship's engineers and three seaman, who took turns in superintending it while in operations. Tents were put up for shelter, and messes formed, and the camp began to assume much the appearance and comfort as possible under the circumstances.

from <u>The Last Cruise of the Saginaw,</u> by George H. Read

Captain Sicard's sketch of his tent. Note the writing desk – this was where he wrote all his naval reports and letters.

From this forward until the arrival of the Kilauea, the same routine was gone through with daily, of working on the boats, with a view to visiting Midway Island, fishing and catching turtle and sea birds. Every Sunday morning all hands were mustered, and divine services were held.

    A part of the story is missing here. We used George Read's account and Dr. Van Tilburg's <u>A Civil War Gunboat in Pacific Coast Waters</u> to pick it up.

    The captain was keenly aware that, by the time they were missed, it might be too late for rescue. Especially as no one knew of their detour to Ocean Island, and commercial ships avoided the area because of the reefs. He devised a plan – one of the boats they had been able to salvage would be modified to make it ready for a sea voyage, and five volunteers would sail to Honolulu to get help.

    This would be a dangerous mission – a journey of well over 1400 miles (the distance "as the crow flies" from Ocean Island to Honolulu). Sicard wanted to know what his officers thought of the plan. He ordered them to each stake out a solitary dune and write down their thoughts, without conferring with one another. One wrote that they were dependent on the condenser for their water supply; the risk of loss of life should it fail (it was not expected to last more than a couple more months) was greater than the risk of sending a boat to get help. Another wrote of his concern about water, and that an outbreak of disease would be devastating because they had little medicine. The ship's doctor and another officer wrote of the risk of disease because of the lack of medicine and proper food. George Read calculated the probability of rescue and how long their provisions would hold out, and wrote that they had no other choice. Sicard's decision was corroborated unanimously, and the sooner a crew could leave, the better.

The boat best suited for the voyage was the captain's gig, a 20-foot open whaleboat. Work on it began immediately.

"Ingenious" hardly gives credit to the Saginaw's carpenters. All they had to work with was what had been salvaged from the wreck. Spikes and bolts were pulled from the debris, straightened, sharpened and reused. Copper was pounded into deck fittings. Lumber was sawed to the lengths and widths needed. The gunwales were raised by eight inches. The Saginaw's copper sheathing was attached to the hull to reinforce weak points. The boat was decked over and covered with canvas. Four hatches were cut in the deck so that the crew could handle the sails, man the tiller, and row. Boards were run under the deck to give the men a place to rest and sleep. The rigging was changed, and new sails were cut.

United States Library of Congress

The crew laying out a set of sails for the gig.

from The Last Cruise of the Saginaw, by George H. Read

Sicard's sketch of her, as seaworthy as they could make her.

Assistant Engineer Herschel Main made a sextant for the crew from an engine room gage and pieces of a shaving mirror. Without it, they would not be able to navigate to Honolulu. Also readied for the voyage were a chronometer, a barometer, two compasses, a nautical almanac and chart, a sea glass and a log-line.

Several men expressed their desire to go, but few actually volunteered. From these the captain, with advice from the ship's doctor, selected the gig's crew – Lieutenant John Talbot, Coxswain William Halford and Quartermaster Peter Francis from the Saginaw's crew, and divers James Andrews and John Muir from the contractor's.

Talbot would be their commander, and their navigator. They would sail north to 32 degrees north latitude to catch the Westerlies (see the chart on the next page), which would push them east to his estimated longitude for O'ahu.

THE MAIN WIND BELTS OF THE EARTH
AND THEIR PREVAILING DIRECTION OF MOTION

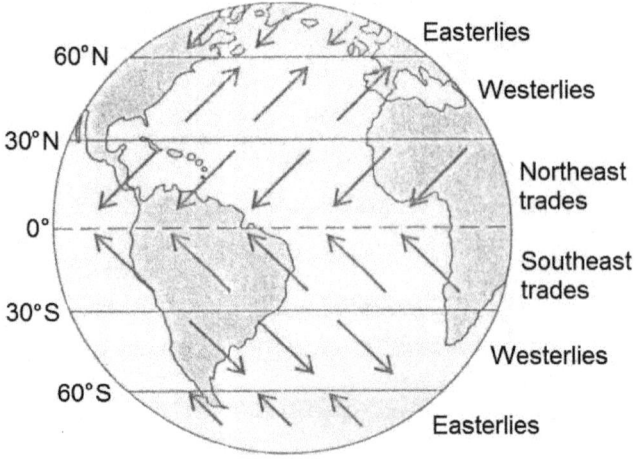

from Marine Biology – an Ecological Approach, by J. Nybakken and M. Bertness

Then, they would turn south and head for Honolulu (O'ahu).

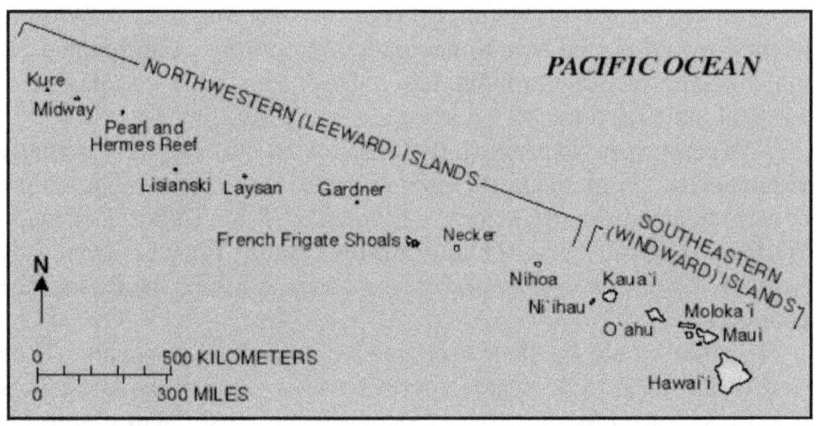

United States Geographical Survey

This would add hundreds of miles to their journey (Ocean Island is slightly north of 28 degrees latitude), but, in Dr. Van Tilburg's words, "… there was no other choice; one had to adapt to, rather than fight against, the prevailing wind patterns and currents for success." They left on November 18, twenty days after the crew had been shipwrecked.

On the 18th of November, Lieutenant Talbot and four seamen volunteered to start for the sandwich Islands, a distance of 1,500 miles, in the Captain's Gig, for assistance. The gig was a fine model, had been a whale boat and was fitted up with the greatest care, and well provisioned. After her departure, the work was vigorously carried on of building a boat, in which to visit Midway, to be forty feet long.

(The boat was to be built to take the crew back to Honolulu, not Midway.)

from The Last Cruise of the Saginaw, by George H. Read

Ripping timbers for a scooner to take the crew back to Honolulu. Sketch by Montgomery Sicard.

RATIONS REDUCED.

The long continuance of a diet of animal food--all the vegetables served being one-half of a decayed potato per diem for each man-- began to tell upon the health of the people, and diarrhea was prevalent.

Medicines were scarce, but quiet and a few days abstinence from Seal meat, turtle, etc., served to effect a cure. On the 8th of December, quarter rations of beans were served out. Fresh fish were caught, but were far from plentiful. December 23rd, the bread ration was two ounces per man; 29th, one ounce of flour and one ounce of beans on alternate days, with a small piece of sea gull, twice a day, varied occasionally with turtle, which were beginning to get scare. With one of the spars a lookout was setup, surmounted by a flag-staff, on which was hoisted the colors, union down, in order to attract the attention of any passing vessel.

December 22nd, 23rd, and 24th, there was a heavy gale from the westward, with a high tide and Heavy surf, which damaged the boats somewhat.

from The Last Cruise of the Saginaw, by George H. Read

The lookout platform, with the flag hoisted upside down (an international distress signal to this day).

November 2nd the Captain, with two boats' crews, were out picking up driftwood from the wreck, when a westerly gale came on and they were obliged to spend the night on a sandpit, in a cold rain. Without a shelter, they adopted the expedient of digging holes in the sand and burying themselves in it. They got safe back to camp the next morning, in a sad plight, however.

RAINS SET IN.

Their anxiety about a supply of fresh water was now past, for the rainy season had set in, and a hole was found which afforded a good supply of palatable water. Life can be sustained for an indefinite period on scanty supplies of the poorest kids of food, but water is an absolute necessity. The sea birds called "goneys" by seaman were not very plenty, and the number taken was limited to eight per diem. No shooting was allowed, for fear of frightening the game away from the island, and the plan was to decapitate them with swords, which was an easy job, as the bird were tame. One swift cut, and the goney make no sign. Eight birds the size of a chicken when plucked, served for ninety-three men.

THE FOLLOWING AN EXTRACT FROM A DIARY OF EVENTS ON THE ISLAND, KEPT BY ONE OF THE SUFFERERS.

--- o ---

SUNDAY, Oct. 30.- The captain took the boats and went out to the ship, returning with provisions and several sails. Those remaining on shore occupied themselves in drying the bread which had been wet in the boats. For breakfast we enjoyed a turtle stew, and supped off "salt horse " **(salted beef)** and hard bread.

MONDAY.- The men and the boats of again to the ship -- a heavy sea breaking over the reef -- after breakfast of salt meat. The occupation of drying bread kept us busy. Our supper consisted of half-starved chickens and turkeys saved.

TUESDAY.- Boat out after drift-wood all day. The boiler of Mr. BAILEY'S engine was got on shore- placed in position, and started as a condenser, to supply us with fresh water.

from The Last Cruise of the Saginaw, by George H. Read

"Boiler set up on the beach and connected with the distilling-coils by a piece of canvas hose. The inner end of the coils was joined to a length of our pilot-house speaking-tube as a return to the beach. By this arrangement the steam passed under the cooler water of the lagoon and was condensed as it returned to a bucket on the beach. Great joy was expressed at the first sight of the little stream and a great fear was lifted from our thoughts."

– George Read's description of Butterworth's innovation, which saved the lives of 93 men
Sketch by Montgomery Sicard.

All hands were joyful over the success of the condenser, as we had been restricted to a half a tea cup of water twice a day. Only two meals this day.

WEDNESDAY.- The Captain and Mr. GARST, who went over the sand-pit after drift-wood did not return this evening; a heavy south-east gale has been raging since 5 o-clock P. M. and we fear for their safety.

THURSDAY.- Still raining and blowing hard. Last night was the most uncomfortable one of my life. Sleeping in rain-water is not conducive to comfort. Capt.SICARD, Mr. GARST and party returned at noon, having burrowed in the sand for a lodging.

SUNDAY, Nov. 6.- Celebrated the arrival of the day with seal stew, salt horse, and one cup of water. A pleasant day. Great excitement was occasioned by a report that a sail was in sight. A boat was sent out, which returned at noon, reporting the supposed white sail to be a white rock on the further side of the reef. Prayers at 10 o'clock, at which all hands were mustered. A cup of water was served to each one at noon from the fifty gallon supply caught during the late rains. Looked over my books and papers, finding the greenbacks all going into liquidation-- quite wet. A brown albatross (goney) on trial for lunch proved most excellent. With plenty of seal and goneys, there is no fear of starvation. May the killing of the albatross not have the disastrous effect on us it had on Coleridge's " Ancient Mariner."

MONDAY.- Capt. SICARD went off to the wreck and succeeded in securing some fragments of sails and part of a mast. Two or three rain squalls during the day. With these and the condenser, we need not die of thirst. It is necessary to dry the bedding each motning, as it becomes saturated with moisture each night. B. and I went inland on a shooting expedition. After an exciting time we killed twelve " boobies " for tomorrow's supper.

SUNDAY.- This morning the ship broke up, and the boats were sent out for driftwood. Fishing party went out in dingy. Prayers at three o'clock. The Captain spoke to the men about the necessity of working on Sunday. The rats, with which the island is infested, have become so annoying that it has became necessary to detail to keep them away from the store-house. It is supposed they were introduced from the wrecked ship

Ocean, lost here many years ago. Last night they ate ten pounds of maccaroni, which we could not well spare.

Rats swarming the dunes.

MONDAY.- To-day we raised the store-house and put it on stilts, to protect the provisions from our enemies, the rats.

from The Last Cruise of the Saginaw, by George H. Read

The storehouse, now elevated in an attempt to thwart the rats. Two sentries stand guard outside. Sketch by Montgomery Sicard.

Friday, 18th.- Tea at 7 A. M. Breakfast at 11 A. M. Gig left at 12. All hands assembled on the beach to bid good-bye and gave three cheers, which were answered by the boat. Had seal, fish and potato for supper. Afthe gig left, the Captain and I took a walk around the island. On reaching the west end we sat down, and watched the gig with my glasses as long as she was visible – a precious speck upon the horizon. On our journey around we saw many seals and birds, but no turtle. We were very careful not to disturb them, as we do not wish to run any risk of their leaving the island. The eggs of the goonies (they are just beginning to lay) are about a pound weight each, and very good eating here, but I expect we shall not get many ; in the event of removing them, the birds may leave the island, a grievous loss to us. We do not know, but I think they lay but one egg every season.

SATURDAY, 19th.- After a calm night, everybody is feeling hopeful about the gig, from its having had such a good chance to get clear, and this morning the wind is moderate and favorable. God grant she may go safe, is the feeling of every soul here. We are, however, to go to work at once building another and larger boat, on the same model, from the lumber brought from the wreck. It is quite calm today, and a party of men are on the wreck ; Nothing left of her but the star-board side of the quarter deck. Ripping off planking, I find myself much weaker from want of food, but as long as I don't work I seem to be as well as ever. I consider myself very fortunate, for there has been dysentery in camp.

SUNDAY, Nov. 20th.-' A bright, beautiful and cool morning, with a good breeze from the northward--splendid for the gig. Everybody is full of hope, but faces begin to look " peaked " from want of food. However, nobody complains, and today there is no work, and prospects of a better feed than usual. Mr. COGGSWELL killed thirty birds last evening. We shall have twenty of them for breakfast, and the remainder for supper, with pork. Mr. BAILEY opened his bible by chance, the day the gig left, and opened it at the fift-first chapter of Isaiah, " The isles shall wait upon me and on my arm shall they trust."

Had service at noon; breakfast at ten, supper at five. We had birds for breakfast, and for supper feasted off birds and twenty-two pounds of pork. The Captain spoke to the men about being careful of the water from the well and warned them to use none of it except for drinking purposes, as it appeared to rise and fall with the tide, and last night was very low.

THURSDAY, 24th.- Twenty-six men on the sick-list, owing no doubt, to the system of meals. I feel the effects of seal eating myself. Am very weak.. After sawing about ten minutes at some planking today was obliged to lie down.

SATURDAY, Dec. 10th.- The trade wind came up at noon, and the weather soon became quite cold. Had a lookout in the cross-tress on the mast in order to signalize the China steamer, should she pass close enough. We are also on the lookout for relief from Honolulu. The potatoes ran out this morning. We were obliged to stop work at noon, the sand cut our faces and eyes so.

THURSDAY, Dec. 22 .- A most terrible gale raged last night. At 3 A. M. all hands were called to haul up the boats. I turned out and found the sea running high, and the water often coming within a few feet of the tents. The first cutter drifted on the beach, and we had a hard job to haul her clear of the waves. The blocking under the keel of the new boat was washed away, and 6 1-2 o'clock A. M. all hands were again called to carry her up to the bushes. The night was an anxious one, and most uncomfortable one, with rain and a fierce wind from the westward. The flying sand, like snow in the air, cut severely. The store-house was started from its foundations during the night, and one tent was blown down. This morning the breakers are grandly magnificent.

SATURDAY.- A dull and melancholy Christmas eve. The ration of breadstuffs-- flour and beans-- was yesterday reduced from four ounces to two ounces per diem to each man.

Christmas Day.- A lovely day : had an extra ration of coffee and a Christmas present of half a cigar from BLYE. Nearly all the officers dressed in their best uniforms. What a cheering sight would the appearance of a ship be to us ! We have about given up hope of a steamer coming to us, yet we look anxiously for some relief.

THURSDAY, 29th.- After to-day, only one ounce of flour or beans per day. It is just two months since we were wrecked. We still work at the new boat, but lack of vegetables is noticably affecting us all.

SUNDAY (New Year's Day).- General muster and church service. The Captain called for volunteers to go in the cutter to Midway Islands, and stay there.

RELIEF EXPECTED.

On the 2nd of January, Capt. Sicard stated to the officers that he looked for avessel to relieve them. He had reckoned the number of days the boat would be upon the passage to the Sandwich islands, and the days' passage to the island, and should not give up hopes until the middle of the month.

THE NEW BOAT PROGRESSING.

On the 3rd all hands were variously employed on the big boat, taking the sails used for tents and preparing them for the boat.

(This was their 63rd day on the island, 33 days after they were due back in San Francisco and 46 days after the gig had left.)

from The Last Cruise of the Saginaw, by George H. Read

The 40-foot "Deliverance" under construction (bottom right).

SMOKE DISCOVERED.

At about half past three o'clock P. M. Dr. Franklin and Mr. Ryan strolled off to the lookout hammock; after looking a short time Mr. Ryan called the Doctor's attention to what he thought was smoke upon the horizon, but the doctor was doubtful and cautioned Ryan not to say anything until he was certain.

SAIL HO !

They walked back to the tents and were talking about it, when the carpenter shouted, " Sail,Ho ! " throwing his hat in the air and jumping down from the boat.

from The Last Cruise of the Saginaw, by George H. Read

"Sail ho!" Sketch by Montgomery Sicard.

All was now confusion and excitement. A person was sent up to the flag-staff with a glass, who soon reported a schooner-rigged steamer heading for the island.

THE STEAMER ARRIVES.

Just at sundown the steamer came to off the island and dipped her flag, and soon after made other signals which satisfied the party on the island that relief had come.

A HEARTY MEAL.

The Captain now gave orders to let the man have full rations of such edibles as they desired, and the night was far spent before the cooking and eating ceased. At daylight the next morning the steamer was not in sight; but soon after appeared, and the boat was manned to send out to meet her.

January 4th.- Captain Long soon landed and was met by Captain Sicard, who welcomed him quite warmly.

RECEPTION OF THE NEWS OF THE LOSS OF THEIR SHIPMATES.

Captain Long, in answer to inquiries, informed Captain Sicard of the sad fate of Lieutenant Talbot and his crew, upon which many an eye was dimmed with tears and the joy at the prospect of relief sadly dampened.

The officers and men then learned the sad facts about the volunteer party. How four out of five of that heroic crew, after a month of strom and famine, found a watery grave, almost within hail of willing succor; and how one, triumphing over famine and shipwreck, unmindful of himself, and only intent upon saving the eighty odd shipmates whom he had left on the desolate island a month before, boldly secured the letters making known the shipwreck, and, exhausted as he was, reaching shore, put them in a very secure place, so that any one seeing the wrecked boat, and perhaps his lifeless body and those of his comrades, might know for what they had sacrificed themselves, fowrad the dispatches, and thus secure the speedy relief of the survivors on that distant and barren inlet. The brave Talbot dead. Sad, indeed, was the news.

THE WRECKED CREW EMBARKED.

On the 5th, at sundown, all hands were safely on board the Kilauea, and she was headed for Midway Island to take in a supply of coal.

January 7th, at half past four P. M., being coaled, the steamer was headed away for this place, and after a pleasant passage of seven days, came to dock.

VISIT OF THE WRECKED OFFICERS TO THE KING.

On the 26th, Captain Sicard and officers of the Saginaw, Captain Glass and officers of the Nyack, and the United States Consul, Mr. Mattoon, were granted an audience by his Majesty the King. Captain Sicard took occasion to thank the King for the prompt dispatch of the steamer for the relief of the Saginaw's crew.

His excellency the minister resident of the United States, on the 23rd inst., having applied for an audience with his Majesty, in order that he might present Lieutenant Commander Sicard, lately commanding the United States steamer Saginaw, Lieutenant Commander Glass, commanding the United States Steamer Nyack, and Calvin S. Mattoon, Esq., United States Consulate at Honolulu. The audience took place on Thursday, January 27th, at 12 o'clock. Lieutenant Commander Sicard on this occasion presented the following address:-

" In behalf of the rear-admiral, commanding the United States Pacific fleet, I desire to thank Your Majesty for the most courteous offer of the steamer Kilauea, to go to the assistance of the shipwrecked crew of the United States ship Saginaw, on Ocean Island. It was a most welcome and opportune relief to the company of United States officers and seamen in distress there, and a proof of your Majesty's friendly feeling towards our navy.

" I am sure your Majesty's kind and humane intentions were most effeciently carried out by the very capable and intelligent officer send in command of the Kilauea, and by his officers and crew.

"I must ask you Majesty also to accept my thanks and those of my officers and men for the sympathy shown us in our probable distress, and for the personal interest taken by you in the speedy dispatch of the Kilauea.

" Your Majesty's minister of the interior also manifested the strongest interest in our relief; and to his energetic and efficient efforts was it due that your intentions werre so promptly carried into effect.

" At Ocean Island we recognized your Majesty's ship as soon as she appeared on the horizon, and our feelings of gratitude may be imagined, perhaps, but can only be thoroughly appreciated by those who have been placed in a like situation to our own.

" On arrival in port, we were welcomed with the most warm-hearted cordiality, and have received abundant proofs of the kind feeling of the Hawaiian people.

" One officer and and four men, belonging to my vessel, bravely and generously ventured on a long sea voyage in a small boat, for the relief of their shipmates;

and finally (with one exception) made sacrifice of their lives upon the shores of the island of Kauia.

" Your Majesty's subjects on that island received the survivor of the boat's crew with great kindness and hospitality, and were most solicitous to recover the remains of my officer, and his men, and to inter . them in a suitable and Christain manner. I desire again to return thanks for all that has been done for the Saginaw's officers and crew."

His Majesty was pleased to reply as follows:-

" Captain:- I am pleased to see you here to-day, and to congratulate you and the officers of the late United States ship Saginaw upon their delivery from their unpleasant position upon a desolate island.

" I am glad that my government has been able to render you assistance. The officers of your service in this ocean have always shown themselves prompt to go to the assistance of distressed men of all nations, and I have lately had a proof of their prompt humanity in the offer of Captain Truxton, of the ship Jamestown, to assist some of my subjects in the Micronesian Islands, and in the efficient aid which he rendered them.

" Such interchanges tend to promote personal and national friendship.

" I sympathize with you, Captain, for the loss of your ship, a misfortune always keenly felt by a sensitive officers, however unavoidable it may have been.

"I sympathize with you for the loss of the gallant officer and men, who, after a long voyage in an open boat, met their death on the shores of Kauia. Such examples of devotion to duty are a rich legacy to all men. Permit me, Captain, to express a hope that you and your officers who have shared with you your service in this ocean for some time past, and your peril in your late shipwreck, may live to attain the highest honors in your profession."

The following gentleman were also presented to His Majesty on the occasion: Lieutenant Commander Charles W. Craven, United States Navy; Lieutenant W. J. Moore, United States Navy; Ensigns James K. Coggswell, United States Navy; A. H. Prescott, United

States Navy.

His Majesty was attended by the chancellor of the kingdom, the cabinet ministers, the government of Oahu,

his Majesty's chamberlain, and Colonel Pratt.

VOYAGE OF THE GIG TO THE SANDWICH ISLANDS - HALFORD'S NARRATIVE, AS GIVEN BEFORE THE COURT OF INQUIRY.

When volunteers were called to go in the gig to Honolulu, Lieutenant Talbot, Peter Francis, Jr., Master, belonging to Manila, and John Andrews, seaman, of Boston; James Muir, seaman, of Glasgow, Scotland; William Halford (myself) coxswain of the Captain's gig, volunteered to go in the boat to Honolulu.

There was put into the boat 10 breakers of water; 5 days' ration of bread, in a tin case, sealed; 10 do., in a black canvas bag, which was mostly spoiled on the passage; about 2 dozen small tins preserved meats; 5 tins (5 lbs. each) desiccated potatoes, to which we attribute being saved from starvation; 2 tins cooked beans, could not be used, caused dysentery; 3 tins boiled wheat, do.: ham, 8 or 10 lbs.; 6 tins preserved oysters; 10 lbs. dried beef; 1 dozen tins Lima beans and peas; 4 or 5 lbs. butter; 1 gallon molasses in keg, leaked out; 12 pounds of white sugar, also lost by wet; 4 lbs.

tea; 4 or 5 lbs. cofferr, both spoiled. The boat was furnished with a small tin cooking x apparatus, by boiling with oil and wick.

FRIGHTFUL SUFFERING.

Five days out lost all light and fire, and no means of making either -- no dry tinder or wood, but had flint and steel. About five or six days before making Kauii we succeeded in getting a light with the glasses taken from an opera glass. Suffered much from wet, cold, and want of food. When we left Ocean Island, November 18, at noon; we run to the north to latitude 32 degrees; there took the westerly winds and run east to Longitude of Kauii, as Mr. Talbot supposed, but it proved ultimately we were not near that longitude by over a degree. We then stood south. Had heavy weather while running eastward; hove to with sea-anchor twice-- last time lost it. Made another drag with three oars, which were also lost. Then made another drag with two oars, with squall sail, by crossing them. That lasted for three turns of bad weather; the last time it broke adrift and all was lost of it. Mr. Talbot was ill for seven or eight days with diarrhoea; got better, but still suffered from fatigue and hardship. he was somewhat cheerful the whole passage. Muir and Andrews was sick two or three weeks. Francis was always well. The deck was leaky. The boat was furnished with chronometer, barometer, compasses, sextant, opera-glass, charts, Bowdich, almanac, barometer. Did not make land so soon by a week as we expected. The first land we saw was Kauhuelaua Rock, near Nihau Island, on Friday morning, 16th of December.

LAND IS SEEN.

Sunday morning, wind allowed us to head S. E. Saw Kauii, a great distance off, Saturday night. Sunday night we were off Haualei Bay; thence hove to, head to N. W., wind having hauled that night to westward. We lay to thus until 11 P. M.-- my watch on deck, called Mr. Talbot; told him night was clear. I could see the entrance to Haualei harbor. He ordered boat to kept away, and steered for entrance, -- got near it, when it clouded up and became dark; have to again to the N. W. At 1 A. M. called my relief; Andrews and Francis came on deck, also Mr. Talbot. After I went below, boat was again kept away for a short time, when she again hove to, it being dark. At a little past 2 A.M. on Monday, December 19th, she was kept away for the third time. I remained below until I felt the boat was getting to shoal water. I woke Muir, and told him it was time we went on deck. He did not go, but I did. Just as I got in cockpit a sea broke aboard, abaft. Mr. Talbot ordered to bring boat by wind. I hauled aft main sheet. Francis was at the helm, and brought vessel up to wind.

A DISASTROUS TERMINATION.

Just then another breaker broke on board, and capsized the boat. Andrews and Francis were washed away, and were never seen afterwards. Muir was still below, and did not get clear until the boat was righted, when he gave symptoms of insanity. Before the boat was righted by the sea, Mr. Talbot was clinging to the bilge of the boat. I called to him to go to the stern of the boat and there get up on the bottom. While attempting to do so he was washed off, when he sank. He was heavily clothed and much exhausted. He made no cry. I succeeded in getting on to the bottom, when I stripped myself of clothing. Then a sea came and righted the boat. It was then Muir put his head up the cockpit, when I assisted him in getting on deck. Soon after another breaker came, and upset her again, she going over twice; last time came upright and head on to the breakers. We then found her to be inside the large breakers. We then drifted towards the shore, at a place called Kalihi Kai, about five miles from Haualei **(Hanalei Bay, Kaua'i Island)**. I landed, with the water breast high, and took with me a tin box on board, with its cover broken, containing navigation books, charts, etc.; also Captain Sicard's instructions to Lieutenant Talbot, and other papers, among which was Muir's and

Andrew's discharge papers, they having shipped November 15, for one month-- they belonged to the contractors, as their employees, previous to that time; - also my and Francis' transfer papers, and accounts destined for Mare Island Navy yard. The above named box, with everything not lashed, fell into water when we first upset. I landed at about 3 A.M, and saw no one till daybreak, when seeing some huts I went to them and got assistance to get the boat into beach. I had previously, by making five trips to the boat, succeeded in bringing ashore the long tin case afore-mentioned, chronometer, opera-glass, barimeter, one ship's compass, boat's binnacle and compass, and also assisted Muir to the shore. He was still insane and said but little, incoherently. He groaned a good deal.. I was much exhausted, and laid myself down till sunrise, when I looked for Muir, and found him gone from the place where I had left him. Soon after I found him surrounded by several natives, but he was dead, and very black in the face. During the day I got some food and clothing from the natives -- one called Peter, and after resting myself Peter and I went on horseback over to Haualei, to Sheriff Wilcox and to Mr. Burt. Then we returned with the Sheriff and Coroner to Kalihi Kai, where an inquest was held over the bodies of Lieutenant Talbot and Mr. Muir, the former having drifted ashore just before I left Kalihi Kai for Haualai. Mr. Talbot's forehead was bruised and quite black, apparently from having struck the boat or wrecked stuff.

from The Last Cruise of the Saginaw, by George H. Read

*Photograph of the gig after her voyage to Kaua'i.
The four hatches can be clearly seen.
Note the damage to the decking on the stern,
and the absence of the two masts.*

from The Last Cruise of the Saginaw, by George H. Read

Another view, showing the damage to the starboard side.

A FUNERAL SERVICE

After the inquest was completed, the two bodies were taken to Haualei, put into coffins, and buried the following day in one grave, at a place where a seaman belonging to United States steamer Lackawanna was buried in 1867. Funeral service were performed by Mr. Kenny, by reading the Episcopal burial service, and two Misses Johnson (daughters of an American missionary) singing.

Before I left Hauaii for Honolulu, it was reported by a half-white who had been left to watch the shore at Kalihi Kai, that Andrews' body had also come ashore, and was taken care of. Captain Dudoit, of the Schooner Wainona, offered to bring me direct to Honolulu, leaving his return freight at Waimea for another trip. I accepted the same through Mr. Bent, and we sailed for Honolulu on the evening of Tuesday, December 20, and arrived at Honolulu at 11 A. M., December 24, bringing with me the effects saved as afore-mentioned. Went on landing immediately to the United States Consul's office, where I saw him and the Minister Resident, and told my story to them.

--- o ---

The death of Lieutenant Talbot closed a career of unusual promise, and in it the navy lost a brilliant and beloved member. A skillful sailor, an accomplished officer, and a Christian gentleman , his self sacrifice has arrested the attention of his comrades, and will remain an example to the service, which in life his virtues adorned, and whose highest qualities were illustrated in the crowning heroism of his death!

--- o ---

REPORTS AND FINDINGS OF
COURT OF INQUIRY.

--- o ---

" The court is of the opinion that the wrecking of the " Saginaw " was caused by a current, as the evidence shows " care in running the vessel at a safe rate of speed, and " the log line was found to be correct two days before, " and had been used only ten hours at sea afterward; and " that Lieutenant-Commander Montgomery Sicard used due " vigilance and care in the navigation of his vessel, " and after striking upon the reef, that he exercised " sound judgement and exhibited great skill and Prudence."

--- o ---

EXTRACT FROM REPORT OF
COMMODORE WM. ROGERS TAYLOR,
COMMANDER NORTH PACIFIC SQUADRON.

" I can not refrain from expressing my admiration of his (Captain Sicard's) industry, prudence, excellent judgement and devotion to duty under the trying circumstanes in which he was placed. It must not be forgotten that when he made the report just mentioned, together with many of those for the Department and Bureaus, and all the memorandum from which the whole mass was compiled, he was shipwrecked upon a desert island, with but a distant prospect of relief.

That he should have found time in the midst of engrossing and anxious duties devolving on him, and should have had the inclination to apply himself to suck work, however important it might be, is a matter of surprise to me.

In my opinion, but few officers would have produced under similar circumstanes such a full and intelligent record of facts and events s is herewith presented.

--- o ---

REAR-ADMIRAL JOHN A. WINSLOW, COMMANDING PACIFIC FLEET, SAN FRANCISCO, CALIFORNIA, reports as follows:-

" I fully concur with the opinion expressed by Commodore Taylor of the arrangement, system, method and application observed by Commander Sicard under the trying circumstances of his shipwreck and exposure, and I would refer to it as an evidence of the character of the man, who under such circumstances was enabled to fulfill all those duties so credutably."

HONOLULU, HAWAIIAN ISLANDS,

January 18, 1871.

Sir:- I forward herewith the brief report called for by regulations, of the death of Lieutenant J. G. Talbot, (and also three of the crew of the United States steamer Saginaw) at the Island of Kauai (Hawaiian group).

I feel that something more is due to these devoted and gallant friends, who so nobly risked their lives to save those of their shipmates: and I beg leave to report the following facts regarding their voyage from Ocean Island, and its melancholy conclusion.

The boat which had been the Saginaw's gig, and was a whale boat of a very fine model,) was prepared for the voyage with the greatest care. She was raised on the gunwale eight inches, decked over, and had new sails, etc.

The boat left Ocean Island November 18, 1870.

The route indicated by me to Lieutenant Talbot was to steer to the northward " by the wind " until he got to the latitude of about 32 degrees north, and then to make his way to the eastward, until he could "lay" the Hawaiian Islands with the northeast trade winds. He seems to have followed about that route.

The boat lost her sea anchor and oars in a gale of wind, and a good deal of her provisions was spoiled by salt water.

The navigation instruments were of but little use, on account of the lively motions of the boat; and when she was supposed to be in the longitude of Kauai, she was really about one and one-half degrees to the west-ward; thus, instead of the Island of Kauai, she finally sighted the rock Kauhulaua, (the southernmost point of land in the group) and beat up from thence to the Island of Kauai.
She was hove to off the entrance of Hanalei Bay during part of the night of Monday, December 19; and in attempting to run into the bay around 2:30 A. M., she got suddenly into the breakers, (which here made a considerable distance from the shore) and was capsized.

I enclose herewith a copy of the deposition of William Halford, coxswain, the only survivor of this gallant crew; his narrative being the one from which all accounts are taken. I have not seen him myself, as he left here before my arrival.

Peter Francis, quartermaster, and John Andrews, coxswain, were washed overboard at once and disappeared. Lieutenant Talbot was washed off the boat, and when she capsized he clung to the bottom, and tried to climb upon it, going to the stem for that purpose; the boat gave a plunge, and Halford thinks that the boat's gunwale or stem must have struck Mr. Talbot in the forehead, as he let go his hold and went down.

James Muir was below when the boat struck the breakers, and does not appear to have come out of her until she had rolled over once. He must have suffered some injury in the boat, as he appears to have been out of his mind, and his face turned black immediately after his death. As will be seen by Halford's statement, Muir reached the shore, but died of exhaustion on the way to the native's huts.

The body of John Andrews did not come on shore until about December 20. All clothes had been stripped from it. The body of Peter Francis has not been recovered.

The bodies are buried side by side at Hanalei (Kauai). The service was read over them in a proper matter. Suitable grave-stones will be erected over them by subscription of the officers and crew of the Saginaw.

As soon as we had gotten on Ocean Island, after the Saginaw's wreck, Lieutenant Talbot volunteered to take this boat to Honolulu, and the rest volunteered as soon as it was known that men might perhaps be wanted for such service.

Mr. Talbot was a very zealous and spirited officer. I had observed his excellent qualities from the time of his joining the Saginaw in Honolulu (September 23, 1870). During the wreck and afterward, he rendered me the greatest assistance and service by his fine bearing, his cheerfulness and devotion to duty. His boat was evidently commanded with the greatest intelligence, fortitude and gallantry, and with the most admirable devotion. May the service always be able to find such men in time of need.

The men were fine specimens of seamen--cool and brave, with great endurance and excellent physical strength. They were undoubtly those best qualified in the whole party on Ocean Island to perform such A service. Both Lieutenant Talbot and his men had very firm confidence in their boat, and looked forward with cheerfulness to the voyage. Such men should be the pride of the navy, and the news of their death cast a deep gloom over the otherwise cheerful feelings with which the Kalauea was welcomed at Ocean Island.

I don't know that I sufficiently express my deep sense of their devotion and gallantry; words seems to fail me in doing justice to my feelings in that respect.

Previous to the sailing of the boat from Ocean Island, I had enlisted John Andrews and James Muir, as seaman, for one month. Since I have ascertained their fate, I have ordered them to be rated as petty officers, (in ratings allowed to most of the "fourth rates") as I have thought that all the crew of that boat should have stood on equal footings as regards the amounts they might be entitled to in case od disaster, as they all incurred the same risk.

Andrews and Muir belonged to the party of Mr. G. W. Townsend,(the contractor at Midway Islands) and it was made by them a condition of their enlistment that it should not interfere with their contract with Mr. Townsend. It was intended as the security of their families against the risk incurred while performing this great service for the shipwrecked party. I have forwarded their enlistment papers to the Bureau of Equipment and Recruiting.

I am, very respectfully, your obedient servant,

MONTGOMERY SICARD,

Lieutenant Commander, United States Navy, Comd'g.

Hon. GEO. M. ROBESON, Secretary of the Navy.

A Missing Ship

The 155-foot steamer and her crew were due back in San Francisco on December 1. On December 8, Rear Admiral John A. Winslow, Commander of the Pacific Fleet, telegraphed his concerns to the Navy Department. "... the delay has made me apprehensive that some disaster has happened to her, and she may have put into Honolulu. Should this have been the case, the next steamer due in two or three days will no doubt bring us the news." And the next day, "Saginaw has not yet arrived." And again the next week, "Nothing has been heard from her as yet." This was around the 16th of December. Halford landed on the 19th, but did not arrive in Honolulu until the 24th. Rear Admiral Winslow didn't learn what had happened to the Saginaw until January 8, and immediately telegrammed the Secretary of the Navy.

The Court of Inquiry

It is because of Dr. Hans Van Tilburg that my son and I finally learned how the accident on the night of October 29, 1870 had happened. And that Montgomery Sicard was the only one to finally figure it out.

Having lost his ship, his career was on the line. Testimony at the Court of Inquiry had established that he had exercised every precaution that fateful night, but he wanted there to be no doubt.

From A Civil War Gunboat in Pacific Waters – Life on Board USS *Saginaw*:

The problem facing the court was a simple yet persistent one: if Commander Sicard had indeed taken all the proper actions (which it seemed he had), and his officers had been diligent in their duties (which it seemed they were), how then did a ship of the U.S. Navy end up running slowly but decisively aground onto a known navigational hazard? ...

Question by the Judge Advocate: Please state your name and rank in the service and where you have lately been serving.

Answer: John J. Ryan, 2nd assistant engineer, United States Steamer *Saginaw,* and was attached to her when she was wrecked at Ocean Island October 29th 1870.

Question by Lieutenant Commander Sicard: After our arrival on Ocean Island, did you see upon the beach a buoy that had been on Midway Island bar, if so, describe it and its situation.

Answer: I had charge of a working party digging for water on Ocean Island and while walking up from the South western point, picked up a small whisky cask, with painted red hoops, with a large "B" painted in white on the head and about two fathoms of buoy rope attached to it. Saw the keg on board ship, it was brought over from Honolulu, and I saw it on board ship at Midway Island.

Question by the Judge Advocate: Please state your name and position in life.

Answer: William G. Loring, was employed at the Midway Islands as a submarine diver and was on board the Saginaw when she was wrecked at Ocean Island October 19th 1870.

Question by Lieutenant Commander Sicard: While on Ocean Island did you find one of the Midway Island bar buoys, if so describe it, its number and situation.

Answer: The day we landed at Ocean Island I found a buoy on the beach and looked at it, it was number VI, and had seen it at Midway Islands, about a week before we left there."

For any buoy… to drift from Midway to Ocean Island indicated the existence of a current setting to the west at that particular time of year. The estimation of a single buoy making the crossing in a matter of a few days seemed to indicate a significant current… But except for some general descriptions of currents in the larger Pacific basin… very little was specifically known about the seasonal currents among the Northern Hawaiian Islands. Ensign Cogswell and his commanding officer had no way of knowing that their ship was being set to westward at a dangerous pace, ending up ahead of their projected landfall by several hours.

Epilogue

The Crew

Lieutenant John Gunnell Talbot and the contractors John Andrews and James Muir were buried on Kauai'i. The body of Quartermaster Peter Francis was never found.

Talbot's body was moved to Danville, Kentucky by his family. He had never married.

The bodies of John Andrews and James Muir were moved to the naval section of Nu'uanu Cemetery in Honolulu, and a single headstone in memory of Andrews (Coxswain of the gig), Muir (Captain of Hold of the gig) and Francis (Quartermaster of the gig) was placed on their grave.

A stone tablet in memory of the four men who gave their lives for their shipmates stands today at the U.S. Naval Academy at Annapolis.

Compensation to the families of Andrews and Muir was stalled. Montgomery Sicard stepped in, and made sure that it was delivered. Andrews left a wife and an eighteen-year-old son. Muir left a wife, and when she could not be located, Sicard hired a detective to find her.

Of the officers who survived the shipwreck – Montgomery Sicard, J. K. Cogswell, Perry Garst, A. H. Parsons, George H. Read, James Butterworth, H. C. Blye, George H. Robinson, John J. Ryan, C. D. Foss, Herschel Main and Jones Godfrey – three (Montgomery Sicard, J. K. Cogswell and Perry Garst), went on to become Rear Admirals.

MONTGOMERY SICARD

Library of Congress Prints and Photographs Division

Captain Montgomery Sicard circa 1891 (about age 55)

When the Saginaw sailed out of San Francisco in 1870, the captain had two children – four-year-old Lydia Ella (1866 - 1950), and two-year-old William Floyd (1868 - 1921). Two years later another son arrived, Montgomery Hunt (1872 - 1942).

Sicard was promoted to Captain in 1881 and served as Chief of the Bureau of Ordnance from 1881 to 1890. In 1891 he took command of the Miantonomoh. He was promoted to Commodore in

1894 and to Rear Admiral in 1897, taking command of the North Atlantic Squadron. He was forced to relinquish his command at the outbreak of the Spanish–American War early in 1898 due to ill health but, upon his partial recovery, was placed in charge of the Board of Strategy. He took an important part in guiding the conduct of the war.

He retired in September of 1898 at the age of 62, and died two years later in Westernville, New York (near Utica).

The destroyer U.S.S. Sicard was named after him, as was a street in the Washington Navy Yard in Washington, D.C.

Detroit Publishing Company - Library of Congress Prints and Photographs Division

Sicard (center front) and the officers of the U.S.S. Miantonomoh

WILLIAM HALFORD

The only survivor at Kaua'i, Halford received the Congressional Medal of Honor for valor. He was promoted and remained in the service, and is buried in the naval cemetery on Mare Island.

JAMES BUTTERWORTH

The innovative engineer who made a condenser out of the contractor's auxiliary boiler to supply the crew with potable water never fully recovered from the effects of exposure on Ocean Island. He did, however, remain in the Navy. He died in 1891, twenty-one years after the wreck, at the age of 50.

HERSCHEL MAIN

The engineer who made the gig's sextant from an engine room gage and pieces of a shaving mirror became a chief engineer for the Bureau of Steam Engineering.

GEORGE HENRY READ

The Saginaw's paymaster was eventually promoted to the rank of commander, principally for his service during the Civil War.

It appears that he began to look for a publisher for his survivor's account around 1880, but it was not published until 1912.

> "...I think that the heroes who gave up their lives
> in the effort to save their shipmates
> should stand as high on the roll of fame
> as do those lost amid battle smoke and carnage."

THE LAST MYSTERY

George Read recorded what Montgomery Sicard did, and even what he said. In the end my son and I felt as though we had met our distant relative, if only for a moment. I was struck by how much he was like my father; although two generations apart, they were members of the same family. And they did things the same way.

All the years I was growing up, we had a summer home in the Adirondack Mountains. By choice we had no electricity, or way to communicate with the outside world. Or even with each other, if we were away from the house. But we had a system. Passed down from one generation to the next. If you were going somewhere and there was no one in the house when you left, you put a note on the dining room table. "Walking to the inlet to fish. Back before lunch." Or, "Taking the sailboat out. Back around 3." Everyone always knew where everyone else was, and when to expect them back.

The captain left supplies in one of the shacks on Midway, should anyone become shipwrecked there. He even left a pile of books. Yet he didn't leave any communication that the Saginaw would circle Ocean Island before heading back to the mainland. And this was the shipwrecked crew's biggest problem. As we've said, when they didn't turn up in San Francisco, a search party would be sent out from Hawai'i. But the would-be rescuers would be looking for them in the wrong place – they would be looking for them in the Midways.

Talbot and his crew left on November 18th. Sicard thought they should have reached Honolulu by December 23rd, 35 days later. Sometime before New Year he started to make preparations to send one of the cutters back to Midway to erect a sign for passing ships, but on January 3rd, the Kilauea was sighted.

Why the captain didn't leave a communication, in one form or another, when he left the Midways for Ocean Island is the biggest mystery of all.

133 YEARS LATER, THE WRECK DISCOVERED

The search for the Saginaw began in 2002, and it was discovered the following year. We will defer to Dr. Van Tilburg to tell you that story, in his book <u>A Civil War Gunboat in Pacific Waters</u>. For it was he and his crew who found it. His account is more enthralling than any work of fiction, and his underwater stills of the wreck are surreal. You can see more photos at https://www.papahanaumokuakea.gov/maritime/saginaw.html.

DESTINATIONS

Montgomery Sicard has given us an idea of what it was like to be shipwrecked a century and a half ago, in the manuscript he left behind. A glimpse through a spyglass, back through time.

But we have more for you.

If you're in the San Francisco area and have a sunny day, head out for Mare Island Historic Park. Be sure to stop in at the museum at 1100 Railroad Avenue (check to be sure they're open before you go - tel. 707-557-4646).

The gig's current custodian is the U. S. Navy, and there is an effort underway to have her moved to Mare Island Historic Park. If you'd like to participate, contact the museum on Railroad Avenue.

Across the water from Mare Island, head for the Vallejo Naval and Historical Museum at 734 Marin Street (tel. 707-643-0077). A replica of the Saginaw's prow sails out of a wall right at you.

Photo by Pyara Bagg Sandhu

THE MONSTER ON OUR COVER

Just a tangle of kelp being swept onto the beach at Point Reyes National Seashore, north of San Francisco.

George Henry Read's Account

Just as we were about to publish Montgomery Sicard's manuscript, we discovered that George H. Read's The Last Cruise of the Saginaw was out of print. Yes, you can get it online, but somehow curling up in front of the fire with an electronic device is not *quite* the same as curling up with a book.

So we decided to reprint it here, in a slightly abridged version – only the survivor's account itself, minus the illustrations (most of which we inserted into Montgomery Sicard's manuscript), the introductory material and the footnotes.

And it finally dawned on us that Montgomery Sicard and George Read were certainly fast friends in life. It is only fitting that their two accounts be published together.

THE LAST CRUISE OF THE SAGINAW

BY
GEORGE H. READ
PAY INSPECTOR, U.S.N. (RETIRED)

With Illustrations from Sketches by Lieutenant
Commander (afterwards Rear-Admiral)
Sicard and from Contemporary
Photographs

BOSTON AND NEW YORK
HOUGHTON MIFFLIN COMPANY
The Riverside Press Cambridge
1912

COPYRIGHT, 1912, BY GEORGE H. READ
ALL RIGHTS RESERVED
Published February 1912

ONE HUNDRED AND FIFTY COPIES OF
THIS FIRST EDITION PRINTED AND
BOUND UNCUT WITH PAPER LABEL

THIS BOOK
IS DEDICATED TO THE MEMORY OF THE NOBLE
MEN WHO LOST THEIR LIVES IN THE
EFFORT TO OBTAIN RELIEF FOR
THEIR SHIPWRECKED
COMRADES

THE LAST CRUISE OF THE SAGINAW

I

THE BEGINNING OF THE CRUISE

During the winter of 1869-70 the United States Steamer Saginaw was being repaired at the Mare Island Navy Yard, and her officers and crew were recuperating after a cruise on the west coast of Mexico,—a trying one for all hands on board as well as for the vessel itself.

The "Alta-Californian" of San Francisco published the following soon after our return from the Mexican coast. It is all that need be said of the cruise. We were all very glad to have it behind us and forget it.

The Saginaw, lately returned from the Mexican coast, had a pretty severe experience during her short cruise. At Manzanillo she contracted the coast fever, a form of remittent, and at one time had twenty-five cases, but a single death, however, occurring.

On the way up, most of the time under sail, the machinery being disabled, the voyage was so prolonged that when she arrived at San Francisco there was not a half-day's allowance of provisions on board and for many days the officers had been on "ship's grub."

Our repairs and refitting were but preliminary to another (and the last) departure of the Saginaw from her native land. Our captain, Lieutenant-Commander Montgomery Sicard, had received orders to proceed to the Midway Islands, *via* Honolulu, and to comply with instructions that will appear later in these pages. (I should explain here that the commanding officer of a single vessel is usually addressed as "Captain," whatever his real rank may be, and I shall use that term throughout my narrative.)

In a northwesterly direction from the Sandwich Islands there stretches for over a thousand miles a succession of coral reefs and shoals, with here and there a sandy islet thrown up by the winds and waves. They are mostly bare of vegetation beyond a stunted growth of bushes. These islets are called "atolls" by geographers, and their foundations are created by the mysterious "polyps" or coral insects.

These atolls abound in the Pacific Ocean, and rising but a few feet above the surface, surrounded by uncertain and uncharted currents, are the dread of navigators.

Near the centre of the North Pacific and near the western end of the chain of atolls above mentioned, are two small sand islands in the usual lagoon, with a coral reef enclosing both. They were discovered by an American captain, N.C. Brooks, of the Hawaiian bark Gambia, and by him reported; were subsequently visited by the United States Steamer Lackawanna and surveyed for charting.

No importance other than the danger to navigation was at that time attached to these mere sandbanks. Now, however, the trans-Pacific railroads, girdling the continent and making valuable so many hitherto insignificant places, have cast their influence three thousand miles across the waters to these obscure islets. The expected increase of commerce between the United States and the Orient has induced the Pacific Mail Steamship Company to look for a halfway station as a coaling-depot, and these, the Midway Islands, are expected to answer the purpose when the proposed improvements are made. To do the work of deepening a now shallow channel through the reef, a contract has been awarded to an experienced submarine engineer and the Saginaw has been brought into service to transport men and material. Our captain is to superintend and to report monthly on the progress made. Thus, with the voyages out and return, coupled with the several trips between the Midways and Honolulu, we have the prospect of a year's deep-water cruising to our credit.

February 22, 1870. Once more separated from home and friends, with the Golden Gate dissolving astern in a California fog (than which none can be more dense). Old Neptune gives us a boisterous welcome to his dominions, and the howling of wind through the rigging, with the rolling and pitching of the ship as we steam out to sea, where we meet the full force of a stiff "southeaster," remind us that we are once more his subjects.

On the fourteenth day out we heard the welcome cry of "Land ho!" at sunrise from the masthead. It proved to be the island of Molokai, and the next day, March 9, we passed into the harbor of Honolulu on the island of Oahu. We found that our arrival was expected, and the ship was soon surrounded by canoes of natives, while crowds of people were on the wharves.

After six days spent in refitting and obtaining fresh food and ship-stores, we took up our westward course with memories of pleasant and hospitable treatment, both officially and socially, from the native and foreign people. Nothing happened outside of the usual routine of sea life until March 24, when we sighted the

Midway Islands, and at 8 P.M. were anchored in Welles's Harbor, so called, although there is barely room in it to swing the ship. The island is a desolate-looking place—the eastern end of it covered with brown albatross and a few seal apparently asleep on the beach. We can see the white sand drifting about with the wind like snow. The next day a schooner arrived with the contractor's supplies and lumber for a dwelling and a scow, the latter to be used by the divers in their outside work. There also arrived, towards night, a strong gale. It blew so hard that with both anchors down the engines had to be worked constantly to prevent drifting either on the island or the reef.

During the month of April work both afloat and ashore was steadily pushed. The contractor's house was set up and the divers' scow completed and launched. In addition, a thorough survey of the entire reef and bar was completed.

Our several trips between the Midways and Honolulu need but brief mention. They were slow and monotonous, being made mostly under sail. The Saginaw was not built for that purpose. On one occasion, on account of head winds, we made but twenty miles on our course in two days.

The last return to the Midways came on October 12, and the appropriation of $50,000 having been expended, our captain proceeded to carry out his orders directing him to take on board the contractor's workmen with their tools and stores and transport them to San Francisco.

We found the shore party all well and looking forward with pleasure to the closing day of their contract. They certainly have had the monotonous and irksome end of the business, although we have not been able to derive much pleasure from our sailings to and fro.

A brief résumé of the work performed during their seven months' imprisonment I have compiled from the journal of Passed Assistant Engineer Blye, who remained upon the island during our absences.

Their first attempt at dislodging the coral rock on the bar was made by the diver with two canisters of powder, and about five tons of rock were dislodged and well broken up. Thereafter the work was intermittently carried on, as weather permitted. During September and October there were frequent strong gales from the west, and on such occasions the mouth of the harbor, being on that side, was dangerous to approach.

After toiling laboriously and constantly for six months, using large quantities of powder and fuse, the result now is a passage through the bar fifteen feet in width and four hundred feet in length, whereas one hundred and seventy feet in width is estimated as essential. A proper completion would call for a much larger appropriation.

During the month of April the thermometer ranged from 68 degrees at sunrise to 86 degrees at noon and 80 degrees at sundown. The prevailing winds during the summer months were the northeast trades, varying from northeast to east southeast.

A cause of much annoyance has been the drifting of sand during high winds, when it flies like driven snow, cutting the face and hands. (This was so great an annoyance that on our first trip to Honolulu I purchased for each person a pair of goggles to protect the eyes.)

Taking into consideration the dangers of navigation in a neighborhood abounding with these coral reefs, the fact that they are visible but a short distance only in clear weather, and that an entrance to the lagoon could only be made in a smooth sea, it really seems a questionable undertaking to attempt the formation of an anchorage here for the large steamers of the Pacific Mail Company.

When the westerly gales blow, the mouth of the lagoon being, as in most coral islands, on that side, the sea breaks heavily all over the lagoon and no work can be done. On one occasion the workmen were returning to the island from the entrance to the channel when one of these gales came on and, as one of them told me, "It was a mighty big conundrum at one time whether we would ever reach the shore."

II

THE WRECK

With the homeward-bound pennant flying from the mainmast head and with the contractor's working party on board, we sailed from the Midway Islands on Friday, October 29, at 4 P.M. for San Francisco. We had dragged high up on the beach the scow from which the divers had worked, secured the house doors, and taken a last look at the blinding sand with thankful hearts for leaving it.

As Doctor Frank, our surgeon, and myself were walking down the beach to the last boat off to the ship, there occurred an incident which I will relate here for psychological students.

He remarked, as we loitered around the landing, that he felt greatly depressed without being able to define any cause for it and that he could not rid himself of the impression that some misfortune was impending. I tried to cheer him up; told him that the "blues" were on him, when he ought to be rejoicing instead; that we had a fair wind and a smooth sea to start us on a speedy return to the old friends in San Francisco. It was in vain, however; he expressed a firm belief that we should meet with some disaster on our voyage and I dropped the subject with a "pooh pooh."

As soon as we reached the open sea, the captain ordered the ship headed to the westward and the pressure of steam to be reduced, as with topsails set we sailed along to a light easterly breeze. It was his intention, he stated, to come within sight of Ocean Island about daylight and to verify its location by steaming around it before heading away for San Francisco.

It should be noted that it is in the direct line of a naval commander's duty, when he is in the neighborhood of such dangers to navigation, to confirm by observation their position on the charts as well as to rescue any unfortunate persons that fate may have cast away upon them. Our own subsequent situation gives proof of the wisdom of such a regulation.

Ocean Island is about fifty miles to the westward of the Midway Islands, is of similar formation, and is the last one (so far as our chart shows) in the chain of ocean dangers that I have referred to as extending more than a thousand miles to the westward from the Sandwich Islands. It was on this reef that the British ship Gledstanes was wrecked in 1837, and the American ship Parker in

September, 1842, the crew of the latter vessel remaining there until May, 1843, when they were taken off.

The "Hawaiian Spectator" for July, 1838, gives the following account of the loss of the Gledstanes, captain, J.R. Brown:—

The vessel was wrecked July 9, 1837, at midnight. One of the crew only was lost, he having jumped overboard in a state of intoxication. Captain Brown remained on the island over five months, when, with his chief mate and eight seamen, he embarked for these islands in a schooner which had been constructed from the fragments of the wreck. The other officers and men, who remained on the island several months longer, endured great suffering and were finally brought off in a vessel sent for them by H.B.M. Consul. Captain Brown gave the following description of the island. "The island is in latitude 28° 22' North, and longitude 178° 30' West, and is about three miles in circumference. It is composed of broken coral and shells and is covered near the shore by low bushes. In the season it abounds with sea birds and at times there are considerable numbers of hair seals. The highest part of the island is not more than ten feet above sea level and the only fresh water is what drains through the sand after the heavy rains."

Charles Darwin has the following to say concerning Ocean Island, which he characterizes as a true "atoll," as distinguished from "barrier" and "fringing" reefs, which are generally formed near the shores of higher land:

I have in vain consulted the works of Cook, Vancouver, La Peyrouse, and Lisiansky for any satisfactory account of the small islands and reefs which lie scattered in a northwest line prolonged from the Sandwich group and hence have left them uncolored, with one exception, for I am indebted to Mr. F.D. Bennett for informing me of an atoll-formed reef in latitude 28° 22', longitude 178° 30' West, on which the Gledstanes was wrecked in 1837. It is apparently of large size and extends in a northwest and southeast line; very few inlets have been formed on it. The lagoon seems to be shallow; at least the deepest part which was surveyed was only three fathoms.

Mr. Couthony describes this island under the name of Ocean Island. Considerable doubts should be entertained regarding the nature of a reef of this kind with a very shallow lagoon, and standing far from any other atoll, on account of the possibility of a crater or flat bank of rock lying at the proper depth beneath the surface of the sea, thus affording a foundation for a ring-formed coral reef.

The evening following the departure passed quietly in our wardroom quarters and in fact all over the ship. Officers and men were more than usually fatigued after the preparations for sea both on shore and on board. There was none of the general hilarity accompanying a homeward cruise. There was also a prevailing dread of a long and tedious journey of over three thousand miles, mostly to be made under sail, and we all knew the tendency of the old Saginaw in a head wind to make "eight points to leeward," or, as a landlubber would say, to go sideways. We occupied ourselves in stowing and securing our movables, and after the bugle sounded "Out lights" at 9 P.M. the steady tramp of the lookouts and their half-hour hail of "All's well" were all that disturbed the quiet of the night.

The night was dark, but a few stars were occasionally visible between the passing clouds. The sea continued smooth and the ship on an even keel. When I turned in at ten o'clock I had the comforting thought that by the same time to-morrow night we should be heading for San Francisco. We were making about three knots an hour, which would bring Ocean Island in sight about early dawn, so that there would be plenty of time to circumnavigate the reef and get a good offing on our course before dark.

How sadly, alas! our intentions were frustrated and how fully our surgeon's premonitions were fulfilled! My pen falters at the attempt to describe the events of the next few hours. I was suddenly awakened about three o'clock in the morning by an unusual commotion on deck; the hurried tramping of feet and confusion of sounds. In the midst of it I distinguished the captain's voice sounding in sharp contrast to his usual moderate tone, ordering the taking in of the topsails and immediately after the cutting away of the topsail halliards. Until the latter order was given I imagined the approach of a rain squall, a frequent occurrence formerly, but I knew now that some greater emergency existed, and so I hastily and partly dressed myself sufficiently to go on deck.

Just before I reached the top of the wardroom ladder I felt the ship strike something and supposed we were in collision with another vessel. The shock was an easy one at first, but was followed immediately by others of increasing force, and, as my feet touched the deck, by two severe shocks that caused the ship to tremble in every timber. The long easy swell that had been lifting us gently along in the open sea was now transformed into heavy breakers as it reached and swept over the coral reef, each wave lifting and dropping with a frightful thud the quaking ship. It seemed at each fall as though her masts and smokestack would jump from their holdings and go by the board. To a landsman or even a professional seaman who has never experienced the sensation it would be impossible to convey a realizing sense of the feelings aroused by our sudden misfortune. There is a something even in the air akin to the terror of an earthquake shock—a condition unnatural and uncanny. The good ship that for years has safely sailed the seas or anchored in ports with a free keel, fulfilling in all respects the destiny marked out for her at her birth, suddenly and without warning enters upon her death-struggle with the rocks and appeals for help. There is no wonder that brave men—men having withstood the shock of battle and endured the hardships of the fiercest storms—should feel their nerves shaken from their first glance at the situation.

The captain had immediately followed his orders, to take in the sails that were forging us on towards the reef, by an order to back engines. Alas! the steam was too low to give more than a few turns to the wheels, and they could not overcome the momentum of the ship. In less than an hour of the fierce pounding the jagged rock broke through the hull and tore up the engine and fire room floor; the water rushed in and reached the fires; the doom of our good ship was now apparent and sealed.

I hastily returned to my stateroom, secured more clothing, together with some of the ship's papers, then ascended to the hurricane deck to await developments or to stand by to do rescue work as ordered. I had participated in the past in drills that are called in Navy Regulations "abandoned ship." In these drills every one on board is supposed to leave the vessel and take station as assigned in one of the ship's boats. I had only taken part in these drills during calm weather at sea, and thought it a pretty sight to see all the boats completely equipped and lying off in view of the deserted vessel. Here, however, no programme could help us. Our captain's judgment and quickness of decision must control events as they develop.

The night was clear and starlit, but we could see nothing of any land. Perhaps we had struck on some uncharted reef, and while strenuously employed in getting the boats over the side opposite the sea we waited anxiously for daylight. The scene was one for a lifelong remembrance and is beyond my power adequately and calmly to describe.

There was at first some confusion, but the stern and composed attitude of the captain and his sharp, clear orders soon brought every one to his senses, and order was restored.

One of the most reassuring things to me at this time was the sight of our colored wardroom steward in double irons for some offense, sitting on a hatch of the hurricane deck, whistling "Way down upon the Suwanee River." He seemed to me far from realizing the gravity of the situation, or else to possess great courage. At any rate, it diverted my thoughts of danger into other channels. He said the key to the irons could not be found. The irons were soon severed, however, with a chisel and hammer, and he went below to aid the men with his knowledge of the stowage of the officers' provender. His confinement was never renewed, for he did good work in the rescue of food.

A few of the more frightened ones had at first, either through a misunderstanding or otherwise, rushed to our largest boat—the launch—hanging at the starboard quarter and partly lowered it before the act was noticed. A large combing sea came along and tore it from their hold, smashing it against the side of the ship and then carrying its remnants away with its tackles and all its fittings. This was a great loss, we felt, if we should have to take to the boats, for we did not know at that time where we were. The same wave also carried off one of the crew, a member of the Marine Guard, who had been on the bulwarks; and whisking him seaward, returned him miraculously around the stern of the ship to the reef, where his struggles and cries attracted the notice of others. He was hauled over the lee side, somewhat bruised and water-soaked, but, judging from his remarks, apparently not realizing his wonderful escape from death.

As the night wore on, the wind increased and also the size of the breakers. The ship, which had first struck the reef "bows on," was gradually swung around until she was at first broadside to the reef, and then further until the after part, to which we were clinging, was lifted over the jagged edge of the perpendicular wall of rock. She was finally twisted around until the bow hung directly to seaward, with the middle of the hull at the edge. Thus the ship "seesawed" from stem to stern with each coming wave for an hour or more and until the forward part broke away with a loud crash and disappeared in the deep water outside. Our anchors, that had been "let go," apparently never touched bottom until the bow went with them.

All that was left of our good ship now heeled over towards the inner side of the reef, the smokestack soon went by the board and the mainmast was made to follow it by simply cutting away the starboard or seaward shrouds. Over this mast we could pass to the reef, however, and there was comparative quiet in the waters under our lee. This helped us in passing across whatever we could save from the wreck, and in this manner went three of our boats, the captain's gig, one of the cutters, and the dinghy, without much damage to them. We also secured in this way an iron lifeboat belonging to the contractor.

As the first gray streaks of dawn showed us a small strip of terra firma in the smooth water of the lagoon and not far from the reef, many a sigh of relief was heard, and our efforts were redoubled to provide some means of prolonging existence there. At any rate, we knew now where we were and could at least imagine a possible relief and plan measures to secure it.

Although the sea had robbed us of the larger part of our provisions, in the forward hold there were still some of the most important stowed within the fragment we were clinging to, which contained the bread and clothing storerooms. With daylight our task was made easier.

A line was formed across the reef and everything rescued was passed over the side and from hand to hand to the boats in the lagoon, for transfer to the island. Thus we stood waist-deep in the water, feet and ankles lacerated and bleeding, stumbling about the sharp and uneven coral rock, until five in the afternoon, and yet our spirits, which had been low in the dark, were so encouraged by a sight of a small portion of dry land and at least a temporary escape from a watery grave that now and then a jest or a laugh would pass along the line with some article that suggested a future meal.

At five o'clock in the afternoon the order was given to abandon the wreck (which was done while hoping that it would hold together until to-morrow), and as the sun went down on the "lone barren isle," all hands were "piped" by the boatswain's whistle to supper.

A half-teacup of water, half a cake of hardtack, and a small piece of boiled pork constituted our evening meal, to which was added a piece of boiled mutton that had been intended for the wardroom table.

After this frugal meal all hands were mustered upon the beach to listen to a prayer of thankfulness for our deliverance and then to a few sensible and well-timed remarks from the captain enjoining discipline, good nature, and economy of food under our trying circumstances. He told us that by the Navy Regulations he was instructed, as our commanding officer, to keep up, in such sad conditions as we were thrown into, the organization and discipline of the Service so far as applicable; that he would in the event of our rescue (which we should all hope for and look forward to) be held responsible for the proper administration of law and order; that officers and crew should fare alike on our scanty store of food, and that with care we should probably make out, with the help of seal meat and birds, a reduced ration for some little time. He would detail our several duties to-morrow. Then we were dismissed to seek "tired nature's sweet restorer" as best we could.

With fourteen hours of severe labor, tired, wet, and hungry, we were yet glad enough to sink to rest amid the bushes with but the sky for a canopy and a hummock of sand for a pillow. In my own case sleep was hard to win. For a long time I lay watching the stars and speculating upon the prospects of release from our island prison. Life seemed to reach dimly uncertain into the future, with shadow pictures intervening of famished men and bereaved families.

I could hear the waves within a few rods of our resting-places—there was no music in them now—lapping the beach in their restlessness, and now and then an angry roar from the outside reef, as though the sea was in rage over its failure to reach us. I realized that for more than a thousand miles the sea stretched away in every direction before meeting inhabited shores and for treble that distance to our native land; that our island was but a small dot in the vast Pacific—a dot so small that few maps give it recognition. Truly it was a dismal outlook that "tired nature" finally dispelled and that sleep transformed into oblivion; for I went to sleep finally while recalling old stories of family gatherings where was always placed a vacant chair for the loved absent one should he ever return.

III

ON THE ISLAND

Sunday, October 30. No pretensions to the official observance of the Sabbath were made to-day. We always had religious services on board the ship when the weather permitted on Sunday, but to-day every effort has been made to further the safety of our condition.

The captain, executive officer, and many of the crew went off early to the wreck in order to make further search for supplies and equipment. The wreck appears from the island to be about as we left it, for the wind has been light and the sea calm during the night.

I remained on shore with a few men to assist in sorting out and making a list of the articles rescued yesterday and to assemble them in the best place suitable for their preservation. We spread out in the sun the bread, bags of flour, and other dry foodstuffs, even to the smallest fragments, and it was early apparent that unless much more food is secured we shall be compelled to live upon a greatly reduced ration and that our main source of food will be the seal and brown albatross (or "goonies," as they are commonly called). Both of these seem plentiful and are easily captured.

The seal succumb quickly to a blow upon the head, a fact we discovered early in our first visit to the Midway Islands. One of the boat's crew, when pushing off from the beach, carelessly and without intent to kill, struck a near-by seal on the head with an oar, and the next morning it was found dead, apparently not having moved from the spot. Its mate had found it and was nosing it about, while moaning in a most humanlike voice.

These seal are quite different from the Alaska fur seal, of such great value for their fur. These have a short lustreless hair, and their principal value is in the oil that is extracted by the few seal hunters who seek them. They frequently exceed two hundred pounds in weight, and are savage fighters if one can judge by the many scars found upon them. We never thought, when, a few months ago, we amused ourselves on the verandas of the Cliff House at San Francisco in watching their disporting about Seal Rock, that we should make such a close acquaintance with them.

The "goonies" also are easy to capture, although they are large and strong and a blow from the wing would break a man's limb. I measured one of them from tip to tip of wing, and it was over seven feet. They are, however, very awkward on their feet, and, having a double-jointed wing (that is, a joint in it like an elbow) can only rise from the ground when the wind is in their faces. Owing to this fact one only needs to get to the windward of them with a club and look out for the wings. We should like to add some of their eggs to our bill of fare, but dare not for fear of driving the birds away. I imagine it would take but a few of the eggs, if eatable, to go around, for I saw one at the Midways that was as large as those of the ostrich.

Fresh water will, however, apparently be our greatest cause for anxiety; for we have secured but a small supply, considering our number—ninety-three. A few breakers or kegs only, that were stowed in the boats, were secured. Rain, of course, we count upon; but to conserve our scanty supply until it comes is most necessary. To-day several wells have been dug in various parts of the island, but the water found in them is near the surface and is too brackish for any use.

The old timbers of a former wreck, probably of the "Gledstanes,"—the "bones" as sailors call them,—lie near on the beach and look as though they would yield us fuel for a long time. Our fire, which was started last evening by a match that Mr. Bailey, the chief diver, had fortunately kept dry, has been constantly going for lack of more lighting material.

Evening. The reef party returned at sundown, reporting a strenuous day on the wreck. We all had a supper of "scouse" (a dish of pork, potato, and hard tack), and before sleeping the camp site was laid out, the sails and awnings which had come on shore temporarily set up, to our greater comfort. Besides the sails and awnings, more food supplies were captured from the after storeroom and a particularly fortunate prize secured in a small portable boiler that had been lashed to the after deck. This had been used by the contractor's party in hoisting to the scow the blasted coral from the reef, at Midway Islands. There were also in one of the wheelhouses of the wreck some distilling-coils, which the engineer's force with our chief engineer successfully rescued after hard labor, for the sea was washing through the wheelhouse with terrible force. The boiler, suspended between two boats, was successfully landed on the beach, and we are greatly encouraged at the promise of fresh water to-morrow. We secured a barrel, also, partly filled with sperm oil, and a lantern in good condition. These two articles insure us a supply of lighting material for the cooking-fire, which can now be put out at night and much fuel saved. Considerable clothing was secured from the officers' staterooms, and I was fortunate enough to find some of mine rolled up in one of the large wet bundles; and a few soaked mattresses and blankets were also brought in. The carpenter's chest, too, came ashore intact, and altogether we feel our situation greatly improved.

Mr. Talbot tells me that they are literally "stripping" the wreck, and nothing movable will be left on it if the weather will but hold good long enough. No one stops to question the utility of an article found adrift; it is seized hastily and thrown out on the reef to be transported later to the island. Pieces of rigging, boxes of tinned coffee, canned goods, tools, crockery, sails, awnings, etc., all come to the beach in a promiscuous mass to be sorted out later.

Monday, October 31. Still at work on the wreck. Boiler set up on the beach and connected with the distilling-coils by a piece of canvas hose. The inner end of the coils was joined to a length of our pilot-house speaking-tube as a return to the beach. By this arrangement the steam passed under the cooler water of the lagoon and was condensed as it returned to a bucket on the beach. Great joy was expressed at the first sight of the little stream and a great fear was lifted from our thoughts. At supper we had a cup of coffee to finish the quarter-ration of food, which was made into a scouse as before. The hard tack needed in making the scouse, however, will soon be exhausted, for, excepting a small quantity saved in tins, it is spoiling rapidly. So to-day I opened a bag of flour to ascertain if we were to have any breadstuff. I found to my glad surprise that, with the exception of about an inch on the outside, it was sweet and sound. The sea water had protected it with a crust. A barrel of beans was also found to be in good condition; so that our pile of foodstuff under the sentry's charge begins to loom high for our safety for some time to come.

Tuesday, November 1. The crew was formed into several messes to-day, and also into watches. Each mess was provided with a tent, that for our mess (the wardroom) being made from the Saginaw's quarter-deck awning. Such of our dry goods and bedding as had been rescued were removed to them, and our little camp begins to take on the appearance of comfort.

The duties of every member of the ship's company have been so arranged that it is hoped and expected that no one will have much time to brood over our situation or the future.

Wednesday, November 2. The bad weather we have feared has arrived. It came on suddenly this morning from the southeast with a high wind and a heavy rainfall, and before we had been able firmly to secure the tents. After strenuous exertion, however, we saved them from being blown over, but were wet to the skin when they were finally safe in place.

Fortunately the wreck on the reef has been thoroughly explored and there is very little material there now that could be of use to us, unless it may be the timbers themselves, to help us in building a seaworthy boat should it be necessary to do so in a final effort to get away. The idea of sending a boat to the Sandwich Islands for relief has been already revolving in our minds, and to-day was revealed by an order from the captain to the senior officers. After a consultation singly with us, he has directed each one to file with him an opinion on the feasibility and necessity of doing so—each written opinion to be without knowledge of the others.

It is probable that the hulk will be considerably broken up before the wind and sea go down, for one can see it rise and fall with the breakers, and occasionally a piece is detached and floated across the reef into the lagoon. As soon as it is safe to launch the boats, the work of securing these pieces will be started.

The boats are now resting at the highest part of the island in the centre of the camp, for even with the protecting reef the sea in the lagoon has been so rough that combers have reached within a few feet of our tents. As I write my journal we are a wet and sad party of unfortunates.

Our captain and his boat's crew must be having an experience worse than ours, however. They left this morning in the cutter for the sand spit near and to the west of us, to collect driftwood, and are "marooned" there in the storm. They can be seen, with the glasses, huddled together beneath the upturned boat. They do not, however, seem to be in imminent danger, and have made no signals of distress; so we expect them to return as soon as the sea abates.

Thursday, November 3. It has been still too rough to-day to launch the boats for work in the lagoon. We have, however, busied ourselves in erecting a storehouse for the better preservation of our food supplies, and to-night have them safely under cover. Last night the rats robbed us of a box of macaroni, and, therefore, we have put our storehouse on posts and two feet above the ground with inverted pans upon the posts.

We made the acquaintance of the rats last night in our tent when a noisy fight over a piece of candle disturbed our sleep. We had seen a few of them before, but did not suppose them to be so very numerous—as on first thought there seemed to be so very little for them to eat. We now found them to have good lungs and appetites, however, and a good deal of thrashing around with boots, etc., was necessary to expel them. We discussed them before we went to sleep again in the light of a future food supply,—an addition to our one-quarter ration,—and the opinion was general that should the seal and gooney desert us the rats would become more valuable. At any rate, they would thrive on the refuse of the food we had now.

The captain returned this morning from his expedition and gives a sad story of their luck. They had to literally bury themselves to the neck in the sand and lie under the boat to prevent being drenched by the rain. During the height of the storm they had one streak of good luck. They found some companions that the rough sea had induced to seek the shelter of the lagoon and beach. They were large sea turtles, and he and his crew turned them on their backs to prevent their escape. To-day we have them added to our food-supply and they are very welcome, notwithstanding the sad plight of their captors when they returned.

We have also added to our fresh water a supply of about fifty gallons caught in the rainstorm of yesterday, and doled out an extra cupful to each person.

Friday, November 4. The sea is rolling in huge breakers on the reef to-day, enveloping the wreck in spray, and we are constantly expecting to see the last of the Saginaw as a hulk. Several pieces can be seen adrift in the lagoon, and the hurricane deck is probably among them. The boats were launched and the mainmast towed to the landing, where it was anchored. It is the intention to have it set up near our camp and to use it for a lookout station as well as a means of flying a distress signal in case a passing vessel should be sighted. However, we do not pin much faith to the idea of rescue from passing ships, for the presence of these coral reefs constitutes such a menace to navigation that they are avoided. Vessels generally pass far to the north or south of them.

Saturday, November 5. The gig was carried well up on the beach to-day and set in a cradle, to be prepared for a voyage to the Sandwich Islands. It is the intention to raise her sides a few inches, to construct a light deck over all, and to fit her with two masts and sails. (Part of the sails were saved with the boat.) In the deck there are to be four square small hatches (with covers in case of bad weather), in which the men can sit and row when the wind is too light or contrary for sailing. From this it may be seen that the perilous trip has been decided upon by the captain. I have no doubt he feels the responsibility which he assumes, and I have great faith in his judgment. Our opinions were handed in to him yesterday, but of course we do not know what their influence has been, but it must be evident to him that all hands—officers and men alike—are loyally co-operating with him in our trying situation.

We learn that Lieutenant Talbot volunteered the day after the wreck to make the attempt and that several of the crew have also asked to go with him. In fact, so many of the men have volunteered that it will be necessary to take the pick of those most likely to stand the exposure, for although we have seen that such a trip was made in the case of the "Gledstanes," it must be remembered that they took five months to build a seaworthy vessel, while our brave boys will go in a practically open boat.

Sunday, November 6. We were mustered for divine service today, and it being the first Sunday of the month the roll was called and each man answered "Here" as his name was called. After that prayers were read by the captain and an extra cup of water served out from the quantity caught during the recent gale. Work was suspended so far as possible, but the lagoon being so quiet it was thought necessary to launch two of the boats and tow in some of the floating timbers. We were overjoyed thus to receive and haul up free of the water a large fragment of the old hurricane deck. We can imagine some value in almost any piece of timber, but in this particular we are confident of securing much material for the building of our future boat, it being of three inch thick narrow planking. We believe we can make one and a half inch stuff from it by rigging up a staging and converting our one bucksaw into a jigsaw with a man above and one below. The blacksmith believes that he can extract a good supply of nails, and in many ways it is evident that we are not going to wait supinely for the relief we hope for from our brave comrades' voyage.

To-day we killed our first goonies and had some for supper. They were very tough and "fishy," and Solomon Graves, once the Saginaw's cabin cook, but now "King of the Galley" on Ocean Island, says that he cooked them all day. Only a portion of the bird could be masticated. However, it was voted superior to seal, the latter being so tough that Graves has to parboil it overnight and fry it in the morning. The hard tack is exhausted, but so much of the flour has been found good that we are to have a tablespoonful every other day and the same quantity of beans on the alternate days as substitutes for the hard tack. A cup of coffee or tea every day for the morning meal. Supper we have at five.

We had a luxury after supper. There are nine of us in the wardroom mess who smoke, and each of us was generously supplied with a cigar by Passed Assistant Engineer Blye, whose chest was rescued the second day; it contained a box of five hundred

Manila cigars.

Monday, November 7. The mainmast is ready to raise tomorrow. An excavation has been made at the highest point of the island, near the captain's tent, and the mast rolled up to it with the rope guys ready to hold it upright. The carpenter's gang have been busy all day in sorting out material for the gig's deck and for raising her sides eight inches.

While the weather is fine, there seems to be a considerable swell at sea from the late storm, and the wreck is gradually, as it were, melting away. To-day a piece of the hull floated towards us and a boat was sent after it. When it reached the beach I recognized the remains of my stateroom, with twisted bolts protruding from the edge where it had been wrenched away from the rest of the hull. I viewed mournfully the remnant of my long-time home and reflected how it had once been my protection and that now fate had turned me out of its shelter. Many of the hopes that were bred within its wooden walls have been shattered by its destruction, and I thought it would be appropriate to bury it on the beach with an epitaph above it showing the simple words "Lights out" which I had so often heard at its door when the ship's corporal made his nightly rounds at the "turning-in" hour. However, it was valuable even in its ruin for building and burning material. Besides, we are not ready yet to think of anything like a funeral.

Tuesday, November 8. I am writing my journal this evening with feelings of cheer and strengthened hopes, for although the fore part of the day was full of gloomy forebodings it has ended eventfully and happily. Our task to-day, as I have said, was to set up the mainmast, and the work was begun immediately after our breakfast. All hands were strenuously employed until noon. First, the mast was rolled into position so that the foot would be exactly over the centre of the hole dug yesterday. Then a small derrick was made to support the mast nearly in balance. With tackles and ropes then adjusted, as all good sailors know how to do, the heel was lowered slowly and the top elevated by the guys, until the mast stood on its foot and was secured upright. It was dinner-time when we considered it safe to leave, and we were glad when it was finally in place, for the work took about all the strength we had.

What was our dismay while we were at dinner to hear the snap of rope and the crash of the falling mast. Everybody rushed to the spot, and it was discovered that one of the guys had parted and that the sand had not been firm enough to hold the mast erect. Luckily the mast was not injured, and the captain said calmly, as though it was an everyday occurrence, "Well, men, we must do it again."

While we were standing about the hole and the captain was directing preparations for another effort, one of the men, noticing the water at the bottom, scooped some of it up in a shovel and raised it to his lips. I shall never forget his expression as he swallowed it. His eyes snapped, his face went white, and broadened almost into a grin, and he seemed for an instant to hold his breath. Then his color came back, and with a wild shout of gladness he exclaimed so that all could hear, "Boys—fresh water, by G———." And so it proved,—soft and pure,—although within twenty feet of the salt water at the beach. Examination showed that there was quite a "pocket" of this filtered rainwater, and that the point where we had excavated was evidently where the island had originally commenced to form on solid ground. We noticed, too, during the afternoon that the water in it rises and falls with the tide of the ocean in the lagoon without mixing. This was explained by one of the officers, who had before seen such conditions, as due to the difference in density of the two waters, and the fact that the small rise and fall of the tide, which is only about twelve inches here, does not create an inrush and outgo sufficiently strong to force a mixture. However, we are greatly rejoiced over the "blessing in disguise" our falling mast has proved to be, and although the supply is probably moderate and dependent on the rains, we shall be able to dispense with the boiler, which has begun to give trouble from rust and leakage.

Wednesday. Blye and I went inland among the bushes and killed twelve boobies for supper to-morrow. Breakfast, pork scouse and cup of water. Provisions got wet from leak in storehouse last night; took tea, coffee, and wet bread out to dry. Several showers during the day. Mr. Talbot went over to the sand spit and brought back driftwood and four large turtles. Supper, salt beef and two dough-balls from mouldy flour.

Thursday, 10th. Breakfast, salt beef and flour-balls. Getting up ship's mainmast for flagstaff and lookout. One boat off to the wreck. Several rain squalls during day, and unable to dry out stores. Supper on boobies and flour-balls.

Friday, 11th. Breakfast, turtle steak and a tablespoonful of mashed potatoes. The mast was again raised to-day and care taken to prevent a repetition of Tuesday's accident. Stronger guys were led to heavy, deep-driven stakes. A topmast was added and a rope ladder to the crosstrees. Work on the gig progressing fast—nearly decked over. Supper, turtle, eight goonies, potatoes, and cup of tea.

Saturday, 12th. Breakfast on fish, turtle soup, and mashed potatoes. Supper, seal meat and tablespoonful of mashed beans. The fish from the reef are voted no good. They are brilliantly colored but strong in taste, and are said by the captain to be similar to the "parrot fish" that is found among our West India coral reefs. Solomon Graves says that the parrot fish is poisonous, so it is decided to leave them out of our bill of fare. Should it become necessary to augment our ration it will, no doubt, be done by adding the rats, and for myself I believe they will improve it.

Sunday, November 13. Ship breaking up rapidly and boats out to pick up driftwood. Had prayers (read by Captain S.) at 3 P.M., and he addressed us with remarks as to necessity in our situation of working on Sabbath. Thousands of rats about. Put extra night watch on storehouse, for fear of further depredations.

Monday, 14th. Same diet as yesterday. Aired all clothing. Work on gig pushing, and we expect to get her off this week. Every one writing letters to send in her.

Tuesday, 15th. Diet, goonies and turtle, with last of potatoes. The gig was launched and provisions sent down from storehouse. Had a long talk with Talbot. He realizes danger of trip, but is brave and confident; gave him my revolver.

Wednesday, 16th. Cup of tea, 7 A.M. and breakfast as usual at 10; turtle and gooney; Heavy sea on reef, and ship fast disappearing, boats out picking up driftwood. Had to take the condenser and all wood high up on the beach. Wind shifted suddenly from north to southeast. Gave Talbot two hundred dollars in gold coin for possible expenses.

Thursday, November 17. Blowing hard from north. Tea at 7 A.M. The gig anchored off shore. Mr. Bailey and I fixed up the well where fresh water was found when mast fell; good-by to the old condenser. "The little cherub that sits up aloft" doing good work for us all.

IV

THE SAILING OF THE GIG

Friday, November 18. The weather has been fine since the breaking up of the storm of the second.

As to work, every one has had his duties portioned out to him, and there is no doubt of the captain's wisdom in providing thus an antidote to homesickness or brooding. Faces are—some of them—getting "peaked," and quite a number of the party have been ill from lack of power to digest the seal meat; but there are no complaints, we all fare alike. Medicines are not to hand, but a day or two of abstinence and quiet generally brings one around again. In the evenings, when we gather around the smoking lamp after supper, there are frequent discussions over our situation and prospects. They are, however, mostly sanguine in tone, and it is not uncommon to hear the expression "when we get home." No one seems to have given up his hope of eventual relief. It has been very noticeable, too, at such times that no matter where the conversation begins it invariably swings around, before the word is passed to "douse the glim," to those things of which we are so completely deprived—to narratives of pleasant gatherings—stories of banquets and festival occasions where toothsome delicacies were provided. It would seem as though these reminiscences were given us as a foil to melancholy, and they travel along with us into our dreams.

Upon one point we are all agreed, that we are very fortunate in being wrecked in so agreeable a climate, where heavy clothing is unnecessary. The temperature has been, aside from the storm we had soon after the landing, between seventy and seventy-five degrees during the day and around fifty degrees at night. We are very sensible of the discomforts that would be ours if tumbled upon some of the islands of the northern ocean in winter.

The moonlit nights have been grand, and calculated to foster romance in a sailor's thoughts were the surroundings appropriate. As it is, the little cheer we extract from them is in the fact that we see the same shining face that is illuminating the home of our loved ones.

Often in my corner of the tent, Mr. Foss and I pass what would be a weary hour otherwise, over a game of chess, the pieces for which he has fashioned from gooney bones and blocks of wood.

Mr. Main has made a wonderful nautical instrument — a sextant—from the face of the Saginaw's steam gauge, together with some broken bits of a stateroom mirror and scraps of zinc. Its minute and finely drawn scale was made upon the zinc with a cambric needle, and the completed instrument is the result of great skill and patience. Mr. Talbot has tested it and pronounces it sufficiently accurate for navigating purposes.

Another officer has made a duplicate of the official chart of this part of the Pacific, and still another has copied all the Nautical Almanac tables necessary for navigation.

I have been directed by the captain to make a selection from the best-preserved supplies in the storehouse most suitable for boat service, and calculate that Talbot will have the equivalent of thirty-five days' provender at one-half rations, although many of the articles are not in the regular ration tables.

This morning the boat was surrounded by many men and carried bodily into water that was deep enough to float her. There she was anchored and the stores carried out to her. Mr. Butterworth, standing waist deep in the water, put on the last finishing touches while she was afloat by screwing to the gunwales the rowlocks for use in calm weather.

There was expended from store-book the following articles: ten breakers (a small keg) of water, five days' rations of hard tack sealed in tin, ten days of the same in canvas bags, two dozen small tins of preserved meat, five tins (five pounds each) of dessicated potato, two tins of cooked beans, three tins of boiled wheaten grits, one ham, six tins of preserved oysters, ten pounds of dried beef, twelve tins of lima beans, about five pounds of butter, one gallon of molasses, twelve pounds of white sugar, four pounds of tea and five pounds of coffee. A small tin cooking apparatus for burning oil was also improvised and furnished.

I had intended putting on board twenty-five pounds of boiled rice in sealed tins, but discovered one of the tins to be swollen just before the provisions were started off. Hastily the tins were opened and the rice found unfit for use. The dessicated potatoes were at once served out in place of the rice, the cans scalded and again sealed.

With the navigating instruments and the clothing of the voyagers on board, the boat was pronounced ready and we went to dinner. There was little conversation during the meal. The impending departure of our shipmates hung like a pall of gloom over us at the last and was too thought-absorbing for speech. Talbot seemed to be the most unconcerned of all, but as I watched him I felt that the brave fellow was assuming it to encourage the rest of us. I had a long friendly talk with him, last evening, during which he seemed thoroughly to estimate the risk he was to take, and entrusted to me his will to be forwarded to his parents in Kentucky in case he should not survive the journey.

All hands have been given permission to send letters by the boat, so all papers, together with a bill of exchange for two hundred pounds sterling, which by order of the captain I have given to Talbot, have been sealed air tight in a tin case. I sent the following letter to my home in Philadelphia, which I will insert here, as it partially represents the state of affairs:—

You will of course be surprised to receive a letter from this desert island, but it now has a population of ninety-three men, the Saginaw's crew. In short, we were wrecked on the coral reef surrounding it, and the Saginaw is no more. We left Midway Islands on the evening of Friday, October 28, and the next morning at three o'clock found ourselves thumping on the reef. We stayed by the ship until daylight, when we got out three boats and all the provisions we possibly could. We also saved the safe, part of the ship's books, about one fourth of my clothing, and my watch. If you could see me now you would hardly recognize me: a pair of boots almost large enough for two feet in one, ragged trousers, an old felt hat, and no coat—I keep that for evenings when it is cool. I have my best uniform saved, having rescued it to come ashore in. We had to wade about two hundred feet on the reef, and I stood in water about one half of the day helping to pass provisions to the boats; then went ashore and spread them on the beach to dry.

We have been living on very short allowance, being thankful for a spoonful of beans, a small piece of meat twice a day, with a cup of tea or coffee in the morning. I am indeed thankful that no lives were lost, and hope to see you all in three months' time. The gig has been decked over and is to start for Honolulu, to-morrow or next day, for relief.

Ocean Island is similar in formation to Midway, but is larger and the coral reef is farther from the land.

We had for breakfast this morning some of the brown albatross or "goonies," as they call them. We shall not want for meat for some time, as there is an abundance of fish seal and turtle, but the flour, rice, and hard bread will not last more than two and one half months.

I hope this will reach you before you get anxious about us, for if the gig should not be successful we may have to stay here until the middle of March. I shall send this in her to be mailed from Honolulu. Our executive officer and four men go in her, and a perilous trip it will be, for she is only twenty feet long and the distance is over a thousand miles. Look us up on the map.

Most of our sails were saved and we are comparatively comfortable in good tents. I am well but hungry. We have dug wells, but found no fresh water. However, we are getting some from a condenser fitted by our chief engineer. Altogether we have more conveniences than might be expected and are in good health generally. I should like to write to friends, but space in the boat is scarce and everybody is writing.

The hour set for the boat's departure (four o'clock) arrived and we were all mustered upon the beach. Prayers were read by the captain, after which final farewells were said and the brave men who were to peril their lives for us waded off to the gig and climbed on board. They quickly stepped the little masts, spread the miniature sails, raised their anchor, and slowly gaining headway stood off for the western channel through the reef. With full hearts and with many in tears, we gave them three rousing cheers and a tiger, which were responded to with spirit, and we watched them until the boat faded from sight on the horizon to the northward.

As I write this by the dim light of a candle the mental excitement due from the parting with our shipmates seems still to pervade the tent and no one is thinking of turning in.

Mr. Bailey, the foreman of the contractor's party, came into the tent soon after we had gathered for the evening. He had in his hand a small book and on his face a smile as he passed it around, showing each one an open page of the book; when he reached me I saw it was a pocket Bible opened at the fifty-first chapter of Isaiah, where Mr. B.'s finger rested under the words, "The isles shall wait upon me and on my arm shall they trust." He did not speak until I had read, and then said he had opened the Bible by chance, as was his habit every evening. Poor Bailey! We all feel very sorry for him. He is a fine character, well advanced in years; and having by economy accumulated considerable money, had bought himself a home, before coming out, to which he was intending to retire when this contract was completed.

By invitation from the captain I accompanied him in walking around the entire island, avoiding, however, the extreme point to the westward, where albatross were nesting. He talked but little, and I saw that his eyes often turned to the spot where the gig had disappeared from view. As we separated in front of his little tent he said with a voice full of pathos to me, "Good-night, Paymaster; God grant that we see them again."

I find that I have so far omitted to give the personnel of Talbot's crew. As stated before there were many volunteers, but the surgeon was ordered to select from a list given him four of the most vigorous and sturdy of the applicants and report their names to the captain. There was considerable rivalry among them. In fact I was accidentally a witness to a hard-fought wrestling-match between two of the crew who sought the honor of going and risking their lives. The defeated one, I was told, was to waive his claim in favor of the victor.

The following letter, which has gone in the boat from our captain to the Admiral of the Pacific fleet, gives the personnel of the boat's crew and other information.

Ocean Island, Pacific Ocean,
November 16, 1870.

Rear Admiral John A. Winslow, Commanding Pacific Fleet.

Sir:—I have the honor to recommend that the attention of the Department be particularly called to the fine conduct of Lieutenant J.G. Talbot. The day after the wreck of the Saginaw, Lieutenant Talbot came to me and volunteered to take one of the ship's boats to Honolulu in order to bring back relief for the officers and crew of the vessel. He has been most zealous and spirited through this whole affair and of the greatest assistance to me.

His boat (by the usual route at this season) will probably have to sail and pull some fifteen hundred miles, and I think some recognition of his handsome conduct would be proper.

The names of the crew are as follows:—Lieutenant J. G. Talbot; Coxswain William Halford; Quartermaster Peter Francis; Seaman John Andrews; Seaman James Muir. The last two are contractor's men and were specially enlisted by me from Mr. Townsend's party for one month. They were men of such fine qualities and endurance that I thought it proper to let them go.

The enlistment was made with the express understanding between myself and them that it did not interfere with their previous contract with Mr. Townsend.

I am very respectfully,
Your obedient servant,
Montgomery Sicard,
Lieut.-Comd'r-commanding.

V

WAITING

Thursday, November 24. Thanksgiving Day—at home; the noble bird, roast turkey, has not graced our tarpaulin-covered table. He has been replaced by a tough section of albatross. Nor was there any expression of thanks at the mess table until one of the officers, having finished the extra cup of coffee served in honor of the day, said, "Say, fellows, let's be thankful that we are alive, well and still with hope."

Last evening about nine o'clock we were given another flurry of excitement over expected relief. The storehouse sentry reported a light to the eastward and in a "jiffy" our tent was empty. Sure enough, there was a bright light close to the horizon which, as we watched, appeared to grow larger and nearer. The captain was called, and I joined him with Mr. Cogswell (our new executive officer since Talbot left) in front of his tent. After watching the light for a few minutes, the captain turned to us and said, "Gentlemen, it is only a star rising and the atmosphere is very clear. Better turn in again"; and he entered the tent.

Sunday, November 27. Last Sunday and to-day we have had divine service led by the captain reading the prayers of the Episcopal ritual.

(Note.—I find nothing but the Thanksgiving note in my journal after the departure of the gig until November 27, other than official entries of receipts and expenditures of food,—the receipt of seals and albatross killed by Mr. Blye and his detail of men; the expenditure being the same with the daily allowance of flour or beans and the coffee for the noon meal.)

Work has been steadily pushed on the schooner. The keel has been hewed out of the Saginaw's late topmast and is blocked up on the beach. We are ripping the old deck planks in two with our old bucksaw and one handsaw, and while it is slow work we can see our boat planking ahead of us when the frame is ready. The schooner is to be forty feet long, of centre-board, flat-bottomed type, and the captain has settled upon her shape and dimensions after experimenting with a small model in company with the contractor's carpenter, who has had experience in boat-building.

This morning about sunrise the camp was roused to excitement by the loud cry of "Sail ho!" I found on joining the crowd at the landing that the captain had ordered a boat launched and her crew were already pulling away in a northerly direction.

I could see nothing from the crow's nest at the masthead, but the statement of one of the crew that he had seen a sail was positive; and the camp was full of a nervous expectancy until nine o'clock, when the boat returned with the disappointing news that the alleged sail was only a large white rock on the north end of the reef that had reflected the sun's rays. As the sun rose to a greater angle the reflection disappeared. An order was at once given out that no one should again alarm the camp before permission from the captain was obtained.

Sunday, December 25. Christmas Day!! Merry Christmas at home, but dreary enough here! Still the salutation was passed around in a half-hearted manner. It is the first day since the wreck that depression of spirit has been so contagious and camp-wide. The religious services, as we stood in the sand bareheaded (some barefooted also), hardly seemed to fit our situation, and the voice of the captain was subdued and occasionally tremulous. I had donned my best uniform coat, which had come ashore when the wreck was stripped, and tried also to put on a cheerful face. No use; I could not keep up the deceit, and I slipped out of line before the service was ended, to change back to the blue sailor shirt and working clothes. I felt that I had been "putting on airs." It has been my first really blue day, for the pictures in my mind of the Christmas festivities at home but emphasized the desolation of the life here.

Strangely enough, Dr. Frank has seemed to a certain extent to be more cheerful than usual. It seems queer that he, pessimist as he appeared to me when he predicted disaster before we sailed from the Midway Islands, should now be the optimist and attempt to dispel our gloom. Some expert in psychical research may be able to discern, as I cannot, why the doctor's belief in Talbot's success should now have influence enough to change my melancholy into a firmer hope than ever.

We borrowed the chart from the captain and followed in pure imagination the course of the gig; and when we folded it, the doctor said that he believed Talbot had arrived at the end of his journey and we should be relieved. Talbot has now been away thirty-seven days, and our several estimates of the time he would consume have been between thirty and forty.

Every afternoon, when work is suspended for the day and we have repaired to the tent, the expression of Talbot's whereabouts is the first note of discussion; as though it had not been in our minds all the long weary day of work.

As the possible failure of Talbot's brave effort begins to enter our calculations, the greater is the exertion to provide in the near future another avenue of escape. So, with gradually weakened strength, owing to lack of sustaining food, the labor we find arduous and exhausting; I, being included in the carpenter's gang on the schooner, realize that fact thoroughly. Yesterday the captain and myself made another circuit of the island, and both were glad to rest on the return to the camp.

The captain has ordered the cutter to be also fitted for a voyage to the Midway Islands. There he intends to have a sign erected stating, briefly, our situation; to serve in case the Navy Department should send (as we expect it will) a searching vessel for us. Twice every day I have climbed the rope ladder on the mast and searched with anxious eyes through my rescued opera glasses the shipless horizon; sometimes with such a strain of nerves and hope that phantom vessels plague my vision. The loneliness and solitude of the vast expanse of water surrounding us is beyond expression. Truly, it is the desert of the Pacific Ocean, and more dangerous than that upon the land, for there are no trails or guide-posts for the weary traveler when the sky is obscured. One might easily fancy that beyond the line of the horizon there exists only infinite space. As the Prince of the Happy Valley observes in "Rasselas," after an ocean voyage, "There is no variety but the difference between rest and motion."

I do not remember the cry of "Sail ho!" during all of our cruising between the Hawaiian and Midway Islands save in the vicinity of the former.

The rats are more in evidence of late. At first small and timid, they are now growing larger and bolder; running about and over us in the tents during the night. We are getting quite accustomed to their visits, however, and, rolling ourselves in blankets or whatever covering we have, pay small attention to them. If we stay here, though, our attention will become more acute; for they begin to loom up in importance as a food supply.

The seal, on the contrary, are growing less in numbers, although great care has been taken not to frighten them away. Also, we have not lately attempted fishing on the reef, for fear of reducing their food. We have been prevented from trying the eggs of the albatross, that their nesting may continue without interruption. They will probably leave, too, when the hatching season is over and the young have been taught to fly.

So far as our present ration is concerned, with the exception of beans, flour, and coffee from which our small daily issue is made, we are situated as though no provisions had been rescued from the wreck; for the captain has wisely ordered that all the rest must be held intact to provision the schooner. So, with all the nerve we can muster, the work on the schooner is being pushed. To-day the frame stands ready for the planking, and the captain thinks that in another week her mast can be ready for stepping.

Last Thursday we had our second most violent wind and rainstorm. It came with hurricane force from the eastward, and the tremendous sea crossed the reef and reached our beach with considerable energy left in it. Our schooner that is to be, with her frame almost completed, was perilously near the waves, and all hands were called. We turned out in the storm and carried her bodily higher up on the beach and breathed more at ease when we saw the seas diminish with the dying wind.

Mr. Blye has been, to-day, our Santa Claus, and with several others I have received a Christmas present of great value. As before noted, there came on shore from the wreck when it was being stripped a box of Manila cigars, and it has been supposed that they were all distributed by the generous owner and had been smoked. To-day, however, Mr. Blye discovered that three of them lay in the bottom of his chest, and to be impartial he divided them into three parts each and doled them out. My present was thankfully and cheerfully accepted, and while I am writing my journal, is passing off in wreaths of hope above my head.

Mr. Bailey and myself have for several days been having the joint use of an old clay pipe he had saved, and we have been trying to smoke the dried leaves and bark of the bushes around us. It is a failure with me. Now much has been said by learned men for as well as against the use of tobacco, but I do not hesitate to testify to its great value in conditions such as ours. It has been a cheering companion to our thoughts in solitude, and a comfort in depression of spirits. I have even seen one man offer his only coat for a piece of plug about the size of a silver dollar.

Sunday, January 1, 1871. New Year's Day—"Happy New Year"! I think no one but the marine sentry at the storehouse saw the birth of the new year or cared to see the new year come in. For myself I hope there will be no more holidays to chronicle here except it may be the one that liberates us from these surroundings. They have—the three we have had here—aroused too many sombre reflections in contrasting those of the past with the present.

Talbot has now been away forty-three days and it seems almost beyond probability that he should have reached the Sandwich Islands before the food was exhausted. There is a lingering hope, however, that some delay in starting relief for us may have occurred or that he may have reached some island other than Oahu, where Honolulu is situated, and that communication with Oahu may be limited. We are "threshing out" the whole situation to-night in earnest discussion between the sanguine and non-sanguine members of the mess.

VI

RESCUED

Tuesday, January 3. At midnight. It is near an impossibility sanely and calmly to write up my journal to-night—my nerves are shaken and my pencil falters. I have climbed into the storehouse to get away from the commotion in the tent and all over the camp. No one can possibly sleep, for I can see through a rent in the canvas men dancing around a huge fire on the highest point of the island, and hear them cheering and singing while feeding the fire with timbers that we have been regarding as worth their weight in coin. To a looker-on the entire camp would seem to have gone crazy. I will tell what I can now and the rest some other time.

At half-past three this afternoon I was working on the schooner near Mr. Mitchell, one of the carpenters of the contractor's party. I was handing him a nail when I noticed his eyes steadily fixed on some point seaward. He paid no attention to me, and his continued gaze induced me to turn my eyes in the same direction to find what was so attractive as to cause his ignoring me. I saw then, too, something that held my gaze. Far off to the northeast and close to the horizon there was something like a shadow that had not been there when I had last visited the lookout. It appeared as a faintly outlined cloud, and as we both watched with idle tools in our hands it seemed to grow in size and density. Very soon he spoke in a low voice, as though not wishing to give a false alarm: "Paymaster, I believe that is the smoke of a steamer," and after another look, "I am sure of it"; and then arose a shout that all could hear, "Sail ho!"

The order concerning alarms was forgotten in his excitement, but as the captain stood near and his face beamed with his own joy, no notice was taken of the violation. He directed me at once to visit the lookout, and I did so, rapidly securing my glasses. By the time I reached the top of the mast I could see that the shadow we had watched was developing into a long and well-marked line of smoke and that a steamer was headed to the westward in front of it. I notified the eager, inquiring crowd at the foot of the mast and still kept my glasses trained on the steamer until her smokestack came into view. She was not heading directly for us, and I cannot describe the anxiety with which I watched to see if she was going to pass by,—my heart was thumping so that one could hear it. I could not believe she would fail to see our signal of distress that waved above me, and pass on to leave us stricken with despair.

When she arrived at a point nearly to the north of us, I saw her change her course until her masts were in line, and then I shouted the fact to those below, for it was evident she was bound for Ocean Island.

The long dreary suspense was over; our relief was near, and I slid down the Jacob's ladder, pale and speechless. The few moments of tense watchfulness had seemed to me like hours of suspense, and it is slight wonder that it took some time to recover my speech. When I did so I acquainted the captain with all I had seen. By the time I had completed my statement the steamer was in view from the ground, and then I witnessed such a scene as will never be forgotten.

Rough-looking men—many of them having faced the shocks of storm and battle—all of them having passed through our recent misfortunes without a murmur of complaint—were embracing each other with tears of joy running down their cheeks, while laughing, singing, and dancing.

I was at once ordered to break into our supplies and issue the best meal to all hands that I could concoct. This I certainly did with haste, and after our supper of boiled salt pork, flour, and beans, finished off with a cup of coffee, I felt as I might after a Delmonico dinner. It was a much-interrupted meal, however, for some one or more were continually rushing out of the tent and returning to report to the rest the movements of the steamer. By the time we had finished supper she was very near and was recognized as the Kilauea, a vessel belonging to the King of the Sandwich Islands. She came within half a mile of the reef where the Saginaw was wrecked and dipped her flag and then slowly steamed away in a southerly direction. This manœuvre we understood, for, as it was getting late in the day, our rescuers were evidently intending to return to-morrow and avoid the danger of a night near the reef. Our captain has ordered a fire to be kept in good blazing order throughout the night as a beacon.

Thursday, January 5. On board the Kilauea (pronounced Kilaway) at sea. It was next to impossible yesterday to make any entries in my journal, and even this evening I have been compelled to ask Captain Long for the temporary use of his stateroom, owing to the tumult in the cabin and on deck; because I wish to record events while they are fresh in my memory. So much excitement and so many incidents were crowded in during the time we were rapidly collecting our effects and embarking on the Kilauea that it is difficult to note them in order.

The Kilauea appeared at daybreak and anchored near the west entrance of the lagoon, and very soon after her captain came to our landing-place in a whaleboat. I recognized in him an old Honolulu friend,—Captain Thomas Long, a retired whaling captain, and as he stepped from his boat, we gave him three rousing cheers while we stood at attention near the fringe of bushes around the camp. Captain Sicard went down the beach alone to receive him, and after a cordial greeting, they conferred together for a few minutes. Together they came towards us apparently in sober thought, and Captain Sicard held up his hand as a signal for silence. He uncovered his head and said, in a tremulous voice, "Men, I have the great sorrow to announce to you that we have been saved at a great sacrifice. Lieutenant Talbot and three of the gig's crew are dead. The particulars you will learn later; at present, Captain Long is anxious for us to remove to the Kilauea as quickly as possible." He bowed his head and a low murmur of grief passed along our line. From a cheering, happy crowd we were as in an instant changed to one of mourning. All the dreary waiting days we have passed seemed to fade into insignificance in the face of this great sorrow.

Captain Long inquired if anything was needed immediately, stating that a generous supply of food and clothing had been rushed on board the Kilauea in Honolulu, and that she had started to sea eight hours after he had been notified of her mission. One of the officers told him that the thing that would best supply a long-felt want was tobacco; so the Kilauea's boat was at once dispatched to the steamer for a box of it, which when opened on the beach was greedily appropriated.

I went off to the Kilauea in the first of the embarking boats, taking the ship's safe and papers that had been stored at the head of my mattress in the tent; therefore did not see the final disposition of articles left on the island; but they suddenly lost all interest to me and, beyond the fact that our water supply was labeled with a sign for future unfortunates, I know but little. The captain tells me that Captain Long demurred at the length of time it would take to bring off most of the government property, saying that his duty to us and to his vessel made it necessary to get away from this dangerous neighborhood at the earliest possible moment; the rescue of life and not property was his object in coming to us. So our food supply and many articles of equipment were collected and stored at the highest point of the island.

When I reached the Kilauea I was served with a good meal, of which I ate sparingly; and, having deposited the safe in a near corner of the cabin, "turned in" on a near berth, boots and all, sleeping through all the turmoil made when the others came off. And so we sailed away at dusk to the eastward, turning our backs on the desolate home where we had suffered for sixty-seven days.

I have learned that a fast-sailing schooner, Kona, was dispatched on Saturday evening under charter by the American Minister, eight hours after the arrival of Halford. Our consul and vice-consul, with other friends, however, prevailed upon the United States Minister, Mr. Pierce, to accept the offer of the Kilauea by the King; urging as a reason that there was no certainty of our being in a condition to await the slow progress of a sailing-vessel; that there might be sickness and even starvation in our party. The Kilauea was hastily coaled and sailed on Monday.

(Note. The Kona was sighted in the offing as we were leaving Ocean Island, and running down to her Captain Long ordered her back to Honolulu.)

On the way to Honolulu, while sitting in the pilot house of the Kilauea, I overheard a conversation on deck between two of the Saginaw's men concerning the superstition connected with sailing on Friday. "What better proof," said one of them, "would you have of its being an unlucky day than in the case of the Saginaw? She sailed from the Midway Islands on a Friday, and two days afterward she lay a total wreck among the breakers of Ocean Island. The gig that went for help also started on Friday, and what was the result? Four out of the five brave boys who manned her came to an untimely end—how Halford escaped is a mystery to me; but I guess he'll think twice before venturing on another voyage on that day of the week." I said to myself that I would think twice, too, unless I was starting under orders.

VII

THE FATE OF THE GIG

Honolulu, January 28, 1871. Perhaps some reader may deem the story of the Saginaw's last cruise complete. I cannot, however, consider it so while lacking the sorrowful story of our comrades' voyage in the gig, with its fatal ending as told by Halford, the sole survivor. Nor would it be less than ingratitude to pass unnoticed the fact of our hearty reception when we arrived here on the fourteenth, well fed and well clothed through the generous exertions of our friends. The King, his Cabinet, and most of the population were on the wharves as the Kilauea steamed into the harbor. The cheers and hat-waving were but the prelude to a most cordial and affectionate greeting when we landed in the midst of the throng. Several of the officers were at once seized upon and taken to the homes of their old-time friends. When I could elude the crowd I was whisked away in a carriage to the Nuuanu Valley home of Mr. John Paty, and there rested in luxury and comfort until to-day, when we are to sail on the steamer Moses Taylor. In recognition of his great kindness as well as to illustrate the comfortable style of the island homes, I insert a picture of Mr. Paty's bungalow.

On Thursday our captain and several officers were received in audience by the King, and in acknowledgment of the great kindness shown us, the following address was presented.

Our captain said:—

In behalf of the rear admiral commanding the Pacific fleet, I desire to thank your Majesty for the most courteous offer of the steamer Kilauea to go to the assistance of the shipwrecked crew of the United States Ship Saginaw on Ocean Island. It was a most welcome and opportune relief to the company of United States officers and seamen there in distress; a proof of your Majesty's friendly feeling toward our Navy. I am sure your Majesty's kind and humane intentions were most efficiently carried out by the very capable and intelligent officer with his officers and crew sent in command of the Kilauea. I must ask your Majesty, also, to accept my thanks and those of my officers and men for the sympathy shown us in our probable distress; for the personal interest taken by you in the speedy dispatch of the Kilauea. Your Majesty's Minister of the Interior, also, manifested the strongest interest in our relief; to his energetic and efficient efforts was it due that your intentions were so promptly carried into effect.

At Ocean Island we recognized your Majesty's ship as soon as she appeared on the horizon. Our feelings of gratitude may perhaps be imagined, but can only be thoroughly appreciated by those who have been placed in a similar situation. On our arrival in port we were welcomed with the most warm-hearted cordiality, and since have received abundant proofs of the kind feelings of the Hawaiian people.

One officer and four men belonging to my vessel bravely and generously volunteered on a long sea voyage in a small boat for the relief of their shipmates. These finally, with one exception, made sacrifice of their lives upon the shores of the island of Kauai. Your Majesty's subjects on that island received the survivor of the boat's crew with great kindness and hospitality. They were most solicitous to recover the remains of my officer and his men, and to inter them in a suitable and Christian manner. I desire again to return thanks for all that has been done for the Saginaw's officers and crew.

His Majesty replied to the captain as follows:—

Captain—I am pleased to see you here to-day and congratulate you and the officers and crew of the late United States Ship Saginaw upon the delivery from their unpleasant position upon a desolate island. I am glad that my Government has been enabled to render you assistance. The officers of your Service in this ocean have always shown themselves prompt to go to the assistance of distressed men of all nations, and I have lately had a proof of their prompt humanity in the offer of Captain Truxton, of the ship Jamestown, to assist some of my subjects in the Micronesian Islands, and in the efficient aid which he rendered them. Such interchanges tend to promote personal and national friendship.

I sympathize with you, Captain, for the loss of your ship—a misfortune always keenly felt by a sensitive officer, however unavoidable it may have been. I sympathize with you for the loss of the gallant officer and men who, after a long voyage in an open boat, met their death on the shores of Kauai. Such examples of devotion to duty are a rich legacy to all men. Permit me, Captain, to express a hope that you and your officers who have shared with you your service in this ocean for some time past and your peril in the late shipwreck may live to attain the highest honors in your profession.

On Saturday last there was held a sale by a local auctioneer of such articles belonging to the Navy Department as we were able to bring away from Ocean Island. Among them was included the gig which Halford brought from the island of Kauai. We were surprised to learn later that the boat had been bid in by a syndicate of our friends for presentation to us as a souvenir. It has been accepted and we are considering plans for its future preservation. I went down to the dock yesterday to see it prepared for shipment, and its sad story was almost told in the scars upon it. Its bow was bound with iron straps and a large gap in the starboard side was covered with canvas. Its wounds seemed almost as making a mute appeal for sympathy, and expressed the struggle it had gone through.

Halford's Story

When we left Ocean Island, November 18th, we ran to the north to latitude 32°, there took the westerly winds and ran east to, as Mr. Talbot supposed, the longitude of Kauai (Kowee), but it proved ultimately that we were not within a degree of that longitude. We then stood south. Five days out we lost all light and fire and had no means of making either—no dry tinder or wood, although we had flint and steel. About five or six days before making Kauai we succeeded in getting a light with a glass taken from an opera glass. We suffered much from wet, cold, and want of food. The ten days' ration of bread in a canvas bag was mostly spoiled; the two tins of cooked beans could not be eaten, causing dysentery, as did also the boiled wheat; the gallon of molasses leaked out, and the sugar, tea, and coffee were spoiled by wetting. To the dessicated potato, five five-pound tins of which were given us at the last moment before sailing, we attributed the preservation of our lives from starvation. For the last week it was all we had, mixed with a little fresh water.

We had heavy weather while running to the eastward; hove to with the sea anchor twice, the last time lost it. We then made another drag from three oars, which was also lost. Then we made still another from two oars and a square of sail by crossing them. That lasted for three turns of bad weather; but the third time it broke adrift and all was lost.

Mr. Talbot was ill with diarrhœa for seven or eight days, but got better, although he continued to suffer much from fatigue and hardship. He was somewhat cheerful the whole passage. Muir and Andrews were sick for two or three weeks. Francis was always well.

We did not make land within a week of what we expected. The first land we saw was Kawaihua Rock, at the southern end of Niihau (Neehow) Island, on Friday morning, December 16th. We stood north by east, with the island in sight all day. During that night and Saturday stood northeast by north, and on Saturday night headed east and south southeast.

Sunday morning the wind allowed us to head southeast with the island of Kauai in sight, and Sunday night we were off the Bay of Halalea on the north coast. We then hove to with head to the northwest, the wind having hauled to the westward. We laid thus until eleven P.M. It being my watch on deck, I called Mr. Talbot and told him that the night was clear and I could see the entrance to Halalea Harbor. He ordered the boat to be kept away and steered for the entrance. As we came near the entrance it clouded up and became dark, so we hove to again with head to the northwest. At one A.M. I called my relief. Andrews and Francis came on deck, as did also Mr. Talbot. After I went below the boat was again kept away toward the land for a short time and again hove to. At a little past two A.M. Sunday morning she was kept away again for the third time. I remained below until I felt from the boat's motion that she was getting into shoal water. Then I awoke Muir and told him it was time we went on deck. He did not go, but I did. Just as I got to the cockpit a sea broke aboard abaft. Mr. Talbot ordered to bring the boat by the wind. I hauled aft the main sheet with Francis at the helm and the boat came up into wind. Just then another breaker broke on board and capsized the boat. Andrews and Francis were washed away and were never afterwards seen. Muir was still below, and did not get clear until the boat was righted, when he gave symptoms of insanity. Before the boat was righted by the sea Mr. Talbot was clinging to the bilge of the boat and I called him to go to the stern and there get up on the bottom. While he was attempting to do so he was washed off and sank. He was heavily clothed and much exhausted. He made no cry. I succeeded in getting on to the bottom and stripped myself of my clothes. Just then the sea came and righted the boat. It was then that Muir put his head up the cockpit, when I assisted him on deck. Soon afterward another breaker came and again upset the boat; she going over twice, the last time coming upright and headed on to the breakers. We then found her to be inside of the large breakers, and we drifted toward the shore at a place called Kalihi Kai, about five miles from Hanalei. I landed with the water breast-high and took with me a tin case of dispatches and letters. On board there was a tin box with its cover broken containing navigation books, charts, etc., also Captain Sicard's instructions to Lieutenant Talbot, with others, among which were Muir's and Andrews's discharge papers; they having been shipped November 15th for one month. (They belong to the contractors, in whose employ they were previous to that time.) This box also contained Francis's and my transfer papers and accounts destined for the Mare Island Navy Yard. This box with everything not lashed fell into the water when we were first upset.

I landed about three A.M., but saw no one until daybreak, when, seeing some huts, I went to them and got assistance to get the boat onto the beach. I had previously, by making five trips to the boat, succeeded in bringing ashore the long tin case first mentioned, the chronometer, opera glasses, barometer, one ship's compass, boat's binnacle compass, and had also assisted Muir to the shore. He was still insane, saying but little and that incoherently. He groaned a great deal.

I was now much exhausted and laid myself down to rest until sunrise, when I looked for Muir and found him gone from the place I left him. Soon after I found him surrounded by several natives, but he was dead and very black in the face.

During the day I got some food and clothing from the natives—one of them called Peter. After resting myself Peter and I went on horseback over to Hanalei to Sheriff Wilcox and Mr. Burt. Then we returned with the sheriff and coroner to Kalihi Kai, where an inquest was held over the bodies of Lieutenant Talbot and Muir, the former having drifted ashore just before I left Kalihi Kai for Hanalei. Mr. Talbot's forehead was bruised and blackened, apparently from having struck the boat or wreckage.

After the inquest the two bodies were taken to Hanalei, put into coffins and buried the next day in one grave at a place where a seaman belonging to the U.S.S. Lackawanna was buried in 1867. Funeral services were performed by Mr. Kenny by reading the Episcopal burial service, and the two Misses Johnson (daughters of an American missionary) singing.

Before I left Hanalei for Honolulu it was reported by a half-white who had been left to watch the shore at Kalihi Kai that Andrews's body had come ashore and had been taken care of.

Captain Dudoit, the schooner Wainona, offered to bring me direct to Honolulu, leaving his return freight at Wainiea for another trip. I accepted the same through Mr. Bent, and we sailed for Honolulu on the evening of Tuesday, December 20, and arrived at Honolulu at eleven A.M., December 24, bringing with me the effects saved as aforementioned. I went, on landing, immediately to the United States Consul's office, where I saw him and the Minister President and told to them my story.

(Note. The reader may remember the incident I related as occurring at the time we were provisioning the gig; the discovery that the boiled rice had fermented and the hasty substitution of the dessicated potatoes. Halford was emphatic to me in the assertion that the potato was the preserver of their lives and that mixed with water it constituted their only food during the last week of their sufferings. The dessicated potato was at that time a part of the Navy ration. It was also called "evaporated," and was prepared by thoroughly drying the potato and coarsely grinding it. In appearance it resembles a very coarse meal.)

Halford has told me of several remarkable incidents which happened during the voyage of the gig and which, although not considered essential in his official statement, would be lifelong memories to him.

Of one of these he says—and I give his own words: "We were scudding before a gale of wind under a reefed square sail. A nasty sea was running at the time. I was standing in the after hatch steering; had the reeving string of the cover that was nailed around the combings drawn tight under my armpits to keep out the sea as it washed over the boat, when I felt a shock. The boat almost capsized, but the next sea lifted her over. I looked astern and saw a great log forty or fifty feet long and four or five feet in diameter, waterlogged and just awash. We had jumped clean over it. It was a case of touch and go with us."

Of another incident he says: "One night I had relieved Peter Francis at the tiller and he had crawled forward on deck. Somehow or other he got overboard; luckily we had a strong fishing-line trailing astern all the voyage, but never got as much as a bite until it caught Francis and we got him on board again. It was a bright moonlight night."

Of another happening he says: "Then, when our provisions had run out entirely, a large bird came and landed on the boat and looked at me as I stood at the tiller. The other four at this time were very weak from want of food and from dysentery; they were more dead than alive. I caught the bird, tore off the feathers, cut it up in five pieces, and we all had a good meal. It was raw, but it tasted good. About thirty-six hours after this, just at break of day, as I was sitting at the tiller, I felt something strike my cheek. It was a little flying-fish. I caught it, and soon a school of them came skipping along, several dropping on deck. I captured five or six of them and they gave us the last meal we had on the gig: for at daylight I saw land—Tahoora or Kaula Rock."

Our captain has made the following report to the Secretary of the Navy, which adds to and confirms the story of the lone survivor of the gig:—

Honolulu, Hawaiian Islands,
January 18, 1871.

Sir:—I forward herewith the brief report called for by regulation of the death of Lieutenant J.G. Talbot (and also three of the crew of the United States Steamer Saginaw) at the island of Kauai (Hawaiian Group).

I feel that something more is due to these devoted and gallant friends, who so nobly risked their lives to save those of their shipmates, and I beg leave to report the following facts regarding their voyage from Ocean Island and its melancholy conclusion.

The boat (which had been the Saginaw's gig and was a whaleboat of very fine model) was prepared for the voyage with the greatest care. She was raised on the gunwale eight inches, decked over, and had new sails, etc.

The boat left Ocean Island November 18, 1870. The route indicated by me to Lieutenant Talbot was to steer to the northward "by the wind" until he got to the latitude of about 32 degrees north, and then to make his way to the eastward until he could "lay" the Hawaiian Islands with the northeast trade winds. He seems to have followed about that route. The boat lost her sea anchor and oars in a gale of wind and a good deal of her provision was spoiled by salt water. The navigation instruments, too, were of but little use, on account of the lively motions of the boat. When she was supposed to be in the longitude of Kauai she was really about one and one half degrees to the westward; thus, instead of the island of Kauai she finally sighted the rock Kauhulaua (the southwestern point of land in the group) and beat up from thence to the island of Kauai. She was hove off the entrance of Hanalei Bay during part of the night of Monday, December 19th, and in attempting to run into the Bay about 2.30 A.M. she got suddenly into the breakers (which here made a considerable distance from the shore) and capsized.

I enclose herewith a copy of the deposition of William Halford, coxswain, the only survivor of this gallant crew; his narrative being the one from which all accounts are taken. I have not seen him, personally, as he left here before my arrival.

Peter Francis, quartermaster, and John Andrews, coxswain, were washed overboard at once and disappeared. Lieutenant Talbot was washed off the boat, and when she capsized he clung to the bottom and tried to climb up on it, going to the stern for that purpose; the boat gave a plunge and Halford thinks that the boat's gunwale or stern must have struck Mr. Talbot in the forehead as he let go his hold and went down.

James Muir was below when the boat struck the breakers, and does not appear to have come out of her until she had rolled over once. He must have suffered some injury in the boat, as he appears to have been out of his mind and his face turned black immediately after his death. As will be seen by Halford's statement, Muir reached shore, but died of exhaustion on the way to the native huts.

The body of John Andrews did not come on shore until about December 20th. All clothes had been stripped from it. The body of Peter Francis has never been recovered.

The bodies are buried side by side at Hanalei (Kauai). The service was read over them in a proper manner. Suitable gravestones will be erected over them by subscription of the officers and crew of the Saginaw.

As soon as we had gotten on Ocean Island after the Saginaw's wreck, Lieutenant Talbot volunteered to take this boat to Honolulu, and the rest volunteered as soon as it was known that men might perhaps be wanted for such service.

Mr. Talbot was a very zealous and spirited officer. I had observed his excellent qualities from the time of his joining the Saginaw (September 23, 1870) in Honolulu. During the wreck and afterwards he rendered me the greatest assistance and service by his fine bearing, his cheerfulness, and devotion to duty. His boat was evidently commanded with the greatest intelligence, fortitude, and gallantry and with the most admirable devotion. May the Service always be able to find such men in the time of need.

The men were fine specimens of seamen—cool and brave, with great endurance and excellent physical strength. They were, undoubtedly, those best qualified in the whole party on Ocean Island to perform such a service. Both Lieutenant Talbot and his men had very firm confidence in their boat and looked forward with cheerfulness to the voyage. Such men should be the pride of the Navy, and the news of their death cast a deep gloom over the otherwise cheerful feelings with which the Kilauea was welcomed at Ocean

Island.

I do not know that I sufficiently express my deep sense of their devotion and gallantry; words seem to fail me in that respect.

Previous to the sailing of the boat from Ocean Island I had enlisted John Andrews and James Muir as seamen for one month. Since I have ascertained their fate I have ordered them to be rated as petty officers (in ratings allowed to most of the "fourth rates"), as I have thought that all the crew of that boat should have stood on equal footing as regards the amount they might be entitled to in case of disaster, as they all incurred the same risk.

Andrews and Muir belonged to the party of Mr. G. W. Townsend (the contractor at Midway Islands), and it was made a condition, by them, of their enlistment that it should not interfere with their contract with Mr. Townsend. It was intended as the security of their families against the risk incurred while performing the great service for the shipwrecked party. I have forwarded their enlistment papers to the Bureau of Equipment and Recruiting.

I am very respectfully,
Your obedient Servant,
Montgomery Sicard,
Lieut. Comdr. U.S.N. Comd'g.
Hon. George M. Robeson, Secretary of the Navy.

In God's Country Again

San Francisco, February 8, 1871. After a pleasant voyage in the Moses Taylor we are again, all hands,—minus our gallant comrades,—on American soil, and the cruise of the Saginaw is officially closed. The officers have taken up quarters on shore, and the crew temporarily transferred to the U.S. Steamer Saranac for discharge or detail as their period of enlistment may require. The gig came with us and will be temporarily stored until it is decided as to her future. We have started a subscription for a suitable memorial to the gig's heroes, and the other ships of the squadron have generously offered their help. The most approved plan seems to be a marble tablet on the walls of the chapel at the Naval Academy, and the captain has made a sketch of one as it would appear there.

(Note. November 1, 1871. The tablet as designed has been completed and delivered at the Naval Academy... I deem it a fitting conclusion to my story. The gig is also to go to the Naval Academy to be deposited in the Museum.)

THE END

APPENDIX

I have been asked several times how it came about that our good ship could have met her sad fate when so recently out of port, her officers knowing the existence of the dangers so near. I have confined my narrative to personal experiences and to incidents of the life under the conditions surrounding us. However, as such questions may arise in the mind of some readers and in order to enlighten them, I set down below some copies of the results from official investigations by those higher in authority.

First: There is the report of the Court of Inquiry held upon our arrival in San Francisco, which reads thus:—

The Court is of the opinion that the wrecking of the Saginaw was caused by a current, as the evidence shows care in running the vessel at a safe rate of speed and the log-line was found to be correct two days before and had been used only ten hours at sea afterward, and that Lieutenant Commander Montgomery Sicard used due vigilance and care in the navigation of his vessel, and after striking upon the reef that he exercised sound judgment and exhibited great skill and prudence.

This was followed later by the Secretary of the Navy's annual report to the President, from which the following is an extract:—

Leaving Midway Islands on the 28th of October, Commander Sicard, of the Saginaw, determined to run to Ocean Island, a small island lying about one hundred miles to the westward of Midway, to rescue any sailors who might have been wrecked there and who, being out of the ordinary track of vessels in that part of the Pacific Ocean, would have little chance of relief from any other source. This expedition, though in the direct line of his duty as the commander of a naval vessel, was fraught with the usual perils of navigation in unknown and dangerous waters, and about three o'clock on the morning of the 29th of October, the Saginaw, running slowly in the darkness, was wrecked on a reef outlying the island for which she was bound. With much exertion and the exercise of much energy and skill, all on board, including the officers and men of the ship and the working party from Midway Islands, were safely landed, with a small allowance of provisions and materials rescued from the wreck. Cast upon the shores of an uninhabited island with scanty means of subsistence, out of the line of travel, and more than one thousand miles from the nearest port of refuge or relief, then it was that the commanding officer of the Saginaw illustrated the benefits of the comprehensive education and strict training which he had received at the hands of the Government and exhibited the high personal qualities which characterize him as an officer. Ably seconded by his subordinate officers of every grade, Commander Sicard took immediately every possible means for the health, safety, and final relief of those who were committed to his command. Whatever could be saved from the wreck was at once secured; measures were immediately taken to keep up the health, spirits, and discipline of the men: fresh water was distilled by means of an old boiler, and everything was organized so that there was no waste of either provisions, material, or labor.

The boat fittest for the service was promptly repaired, provisioned, and equipped, as far as might be, for the perilous voyage. Manned by one officer and four men, all of whom volunteered for the service, it was dispatched to Honolulu, the nearest port from which relief could be expected. After her departure work was vigorously pushed on the island; and when finally rescued, the shipwrecked marines with well-directed labor had almost completed, from the material of their old ship, a new schooner perfectly seaworthy and sufficient, under favorable circumstances, to carry the whole shipwrecked party to a port of safety. I have thus collated some of the facts of this case to illustrate my high opinion of the energy and ability displayed by Commander Sicard and his comrades on this occasion and to show how well such conduct repays the favor of the Government.

After relating the history of the boat's voyage which we have already read, the Secretary concludes as follows:—

The death of Lieutenant Talbot closed a career of unusual promise, and in it the Navy lost a brilliant and beloved member. A skillful sailor, an accomplished officer, and a Christian gentleman, his self-sacrifice has arrested the attention of his comrades and will remain an example to the Service which in life his virtues adorned and whose highest qualities were illustrated in the crowning heroism of his death. His comrades of humbler rank will not be forgotten; with him they faced the dangers of the lonely ocean and offered their lives with his to save their shipwrecked messmates, and no one can estimate how much of danger and suffering, perhaps death, was saved through the courage and endurance of the sole survivor of that gallant boat's crew.

INDEX, BY CREWMEMBER

Agarrie, Joseph A.	10
Bailey, George A.	11, 45, 52, 107, 114, 118, 123
Bailey, Joseph A.	10
Barton, Nicholas	10
Battersby, Joseph	11
Blye, H. C.	9, 23, 54, 87, 97, 111, 113, 120, 123
Brennan, D. G.	11
Brown, Charles	10
Brown, John	11
Butterworth, James	9, 14, 23, 46, 87, 90, 116
Cahill, Edward	11
Cairns, William	10
Clark, Henry B.	10
Coburg, Lorenzo	10
Cogswell, J. K.	9, 52, 64, 86, 87
Collins, Charles	11
Collins, Daniel	10
Combs, William	10
Daley, John	10
Doran, Martin	10
Downs, John	10
Edman, William	10
Evans, W. J.	10
Fallon, William	10
Fitzgerald, Dennis A.	10
Foschack, James	10

Foss, C. D.	9, 23, 87, 115 (the author of Sicard's manuscript lists him as "C. D. Ross")
Francis, Peter	10, 14, 15, 39, 66, 68, 69, 71, 81, 82, 87, 119, 132, 133, 134, 136
Frank, Adam	11, 23, 57, 99, 121 (the author of Sicard's manuscript calls him "Dr. Franklin")
Garst, Perry	9, 46, 47, 87
Garvey, Michael	10
Godfrey, Jones	9, 87 (the author of Sicard's manuscript lists him as "James Godfrey")
Graves, Solomon	10, 111, 114
Hale, Charles	10
Halford, William	10, 14, 15, 39, 66, 81, 90, 119, 128, 129, 131, 134, 135, 136
Hayes, Dennis M.	10
Hayes, Thomas	10
Hubert, George	10
James, Edward	10
Jones, Thomas	11
Jordan, Michael	10
Judd, E. P.	11
Kearney, Thomas	10
Lane, John	10
Larkin, Thomas	10
Logan, J. M.	10
Loring, William G.	11, 86
Lynch, Michael	10
Main, Herschel	9, 14, 23, 39, 87, 90, 115

Martin, Charles A.	10
McCabe, L.	10
McGrath, John	11
McLaughlin, Joseph	10
McNamara, James	10
Melody, Thomas	10
Miller, J. R.	10
Mitchell, Charles H.	11, 125
Moore, John G.	10
Morris, Phillip	10
Muir, David	11
Muir, James	11, 16, 66, 68, 69, 70, 71, 72, 81, 83, 84, 87, 119, 131, 132, 133, 135, 137
Murphy, John	10
Myfinger, A. E.	10
Nichols, James	10
Nolan, James M.	10
O'Brien, Edward	10
Parsons, A. H.	9, 23, 87
Peck, Lewis	11
Quigley, Frank	11
Riley, John	10
Robinson, George H.	9, 23, 87
Ross, Joseph	10
Russell, J. Henry	11
Ryan, John J.	9, 57, 85, 87
Sarsfield, James	11
Saunders, George	10

Scott, Francis	10
Talbot, John G.	9, 13, 14, 23, 39, 41, 59, 60, 66-70, 72, 75, 79, 81-3, 87, 91, 108, 111, 113, 114, 116, 117, 119, 120-122, 124, 127, 131-133, 135, 136, 140
Thompson, Samuel A.	10
Toumey, Jon C.	11
Vivian, Henry D.	10
Wallace, Henry	10
Wallace, John H.	10
Wauchoss, George D.	10
White, George	10
Wiseman, Thomas	11

www.ingramcontent.com/pod-product-compliance
Lightning Source LLC
LaVergne TN
LVHW011421080426
835512LV00005B/195